Railway Developments Around Leeds and Bradford Since 1968

Acknowledgements

The Author wishes to thank the West Yorkshire Archive Service for their assistance in the preparation of this book. Also Colour-Rail and J.W. Holroyd for providing illustrations. All uncredited photos were taken by the author.

Front Cover: In the early days of East Coast electrification into Leeds, a special from King's Cross runs in behind a Class 86/2 loco – a rare type to visit Leeds. Parcels vans occupying the old 'Wellington' section were still a common sight at this time. (*18 February 1989*)

Rear Cover (top): The d.m.u.'s replacements had, in fact, already been retired! When photographed, this Class 308 was 36 years old, though looking smart in its Metro livery on a Skipton/Bradford service. (*November 1997*)

Rear Cover (bottom): Bradford Forster Square; two tracks still run into the old platforms 1 & 2, whilst the new, long, island platform (to become numbers 1 & 2) has yet to be finished. A new, short, platform 3 will eventually emerge from behind the right-hand vegetation. Bradford Cathedral (with flag) catches the sun. (*7 April 1990*)

Frontispiece: Part of the old Bradford Exchange concourse with step-access to the adjacent thoroughfares Drake Street and Leeds Road at a lower level. Note the North Eastern Region tangerine signage. (*17 August 1972*)

Railway Developments Around Leeds and Bradford Since 1968

Dave Peel

PEN & SWORD
TRANSPORT

First published in Great Britain in 2017 by
Pen & Sword Transport
an imprint of
Pen & Sword Books Ltd
47 Church Street
Barnsley
South Yorkshire
S70 2AS

ISBN 978 1 47388 313 0

A CIP catalogue record for this book is available from the British Library

Typeset in Ehrhardt by
Mac Style Ltd, Bridlington, East Yorkshire
Printed and bound in China by Imago

Pen & Sword Books Ltd incorporates the imprints of Pen & Sword Archaeology, Atlas, Aviation, Battleground, Discovery, Family History, History, Maritime, Military, Naval, Politics, Railways, Select, Transport, True Crime, and Fiction, Frontline Books, Leo Cooper, Praetorian Press, Seaforth Publishing and Wharncliffe.

For a complete list of Pen & Sword titles please contact
PEN & SWORD BOOKS LIMITED
47 Church Street, Barnsley, South Yorkshire, S70 2AS, England
E-mail: enquiries@pen-and-sword.co.uk
Website: www.pen-and-sword.co.uk

Contents

Introduction

Why 1968? Principally because this book is about the post-steam era. Scheduled steam services of the 1950s and 1960s around Leeds and Bradford are well covered (in black & white) elsewhere, and although BR steam did not finish entirely until August 1968, very little of what was left in the north-west of England appeared in the West Riding during 1968. Against this it is of course true that the Keighley & Worth Valley Railway opened on 29 June 1968, thus reintroducing steam to Airedale on a permanent basis, but preserved railways (KWVR, Middleton Railway or Kirklees Light Railway) are not the focus of this book, though these lines will gain a well-deserved passing mention in the appropriate place. On the other hand, main line steam excursions did continue to pass through, or originate in, the Leeds/Bradford area from time to time – especially in the 1980s – mostly bound for the Settle & Carlisle scenic route, and several of these are illustrated in the local area!

In the years leading up to 1968 much had happened to the railway system around Leeds and Bradford (and more generally in the West Riding) that was negative, with the Beeching Report of 1963 forecasting the closure of many local stations, and some entire stretches of line, that fed traffic into these two major cities. The closures covered both passenger and freight services and the majority of these took place in the period 1965/66/67, together with substantial

downsizing of the railway infrastructure in terms of sidings, goods yards and reduced signalling as 4-track sections became 2-track (or double track became single). Not only did many staff lose their jobs at the stations and goods facilities that closed, but even at those stations that remained open, job numbers were reduced, or the stations became unstaffed halts.

All this is familiar background and was repeated to a greater or lesser extent throughout much of the UK, but it was not all negative. The first diesel multiple units (d.m.u.s) had been introduced on services into and out of Leeds (Central) and Bradford (Exchange) back in 1954 and had increased patronage considerably since that time. As more routes gained these new diesel trains, so passenger numbers went up on these services as well – a promising development to buck the downward trend. More and more long-distance trains were, by the late 1960s, also diesel-hauled with (slightly) newer coaching stock on (slightly) faster schedules; Cross-Country multiple units had been running on the busy Hull/Leeds/Manchester/Liverpool route since 1961, and all these developments had proved popular.

However, many of the West Riding stations had seen few improvements to them since they were built in Victorian times, and it was no real surprise that seven of the eight stations on the Airedale line connecting Leeds and Bradford (Forster Square) were Beeching closures (only Shipley remaining open), and all six stations closed on the Leeds (Central)/Bradford (Exchange) route, including the Pudsey loop. On this shorter line, Stanningley was effectively replaced on 6 March 1967 by New Pudsey, a staffed park-way style station which was, in this sense, ahead of its time.

It had long been apparent that Leeds (Central) was overdue for closure and that this, coupled with the transfer of its traffic to Leeds (City), was an obvious way forward. Back in 1957 a £4½ million plan was therefore put forward by BR to enlarge and reconfigure City Station, not only to cope with Central's traffic but to build in extra capacity for future growth. Work began in late 1959 but was halted in 1961 when government finance was temporarily withdrawn. The original plan had included two extra tracks at the 4-track western approaches, plus a flyover to bring Central's trains down to City's level, so a cheaper and less ambitious £2¾ million scheme was substituted – without the flyover and the extra tracks at the western approaches – and work restarted in 1963. It was this smaller project that was completed on 1 May 1967 with City now dealing with all trains, Central having finally closed on 29 April.

By 1968 it appeared that the storm of changes resulting from the Beeching Report had passed, and the railways around Leeds and Bradford could be left to bed-in the new timetables and build up whatever traffic they could muster. However, the most significant event of the year – in respect of its long-term consequences – was the passing of the 1968 Transport Act. In this was introduced the concept of the social (or subsidised) railway, wherein the government and/ or the local authorities could, if they so desired, keep services going and/or improve them out of their own money if the line was loss-making but considered worthy of support (i.e. subsidy) as a social necessity. The provisions of this Act were to be a useful tool in a few years time when Local Government Reorganisation came in in 1972. Two years after this, when the old West Riding disappeared and the area it covered effectively split into West Yorkshire and South Yorkshire, the West Yorkshire Passenger Transport Executive was set up.

Thanks largely to this body (and its successor from 2014 the West Yorkshire Combined Authority), plus the willingness of local authorities to contribute, numerous stations have, over the years, been added to the commuter network within West Yorkshire, and more are still planned. Some of these have been new stations on the sites of old ones closed in the Beeching era, some are on completely new locations where no station had previously existed. As three of the local passenger routes emanating from Leeds or Bradford overlap into North Yorkshire (i.e. to Skipton, to Harrogate and to York), the WYCA has a continued interest in promoting new stations both within West Yorkshire and outside this boundary, as had its predecessor. These successful developments are included later in this book and all the added stations are illustrated.

Over a time frame of 40–50 years it is to be expected that the railway scene will alter substantially, especially in large urban areas. At the beginning of this period, Leeds (City) had only just been rebuilt to handle extra trains following the closure and demolition of Central in 1967, though in the process City Station had lost the six terminal platforms of the ex-LMS Wellington section, which were turned over to parcels traffic and some car parking. (Some tracks here remained intact and were used to receive and despatch the parcels trains themselves; the remaining area was levelled and surfaced so that incoming/outgoing parcels could be sorted and arrive and depart by road.) In general, however, it was expected that City Station should be able to manage any rising traffic levels for several years.

Bradford (Forster Square) was also in reasonable condition in 1968 and had capacity to spare, with very few passenger services remaining, though the station was still busy with heavy flows of parcels traffic. Additionally the station had been partially rebuilt only fifteen years or so previously. In contrast, Bradford (Exchange) was in need of major refurbishment. Here this station was also operating at well below capacity, though still running all the Leeds local trains plus Calder Valley services and all the London expresses from that city. Like Leeds (Central) a few years earlier, Exchange was a prime candidate for considerable improvement, or preferably demolition and replacement as, unlike Leeds (Central), its traffic could not be merged with Bradford's other station.

Demolition is therefore what it got; commencing in 1972 Exchange was replaced, the new station forming part of Bradford's Transport Interchange, to be opened as such in 1977 once the bus station was also completed. Forster Square on the other hand was vastly underused, particularly when the parcels traffic dwindled and the large Goods Depot closed in 1984, meaning that so much land became available as to make commercial development of this space the only sensible option. And so it was that Forster Square was also replaced by a smaller, more appropriate facility, this opening in 1990.

The Bradford stations were both termini and departure lines were solely northbound (Forster Square) or southbound (Exchange). Traffic was light or moderate at both and the replacement stations were provided with only 3 and 4 platforms respectively, against 6 and 10 previously. Having totally replaced both of Bradford's stations within twenty years, any future rebuild of Leeds

station – should this be deemed necessary – would, however, be an entirely different matter, with the position of this station imposing severe physical constraints. However, by the end of the 1980s Leeds was operating at capacity, and the East Coast main line from King's Cross was now electrified into Leeds. With further electrification of local commuter routes planned, extra platforms were essential if the estimated growth in passenger numbers proved accurate.

This book is therefore centred around the total replacement of the two Bradford stations, and the *in situ* rebuild of the much larger and busier Leeds station, and these events are copiously illustrated. Not exclusively however. In 1968 the first station out of Leeds westbound towards Keighley and Skipton was then Shipley, the junction for Forster Square/Keighley and Forster Square/Ilkley trains. With some Leeds/Skipton services calling here as well (by reversing in and out of the triangular junction), this station was already quite busy despite having lost the direct Forster Square/ Leeds local trains. The in/out reversal of the Leeds connections was not, however, a manoeuvre that found favour with the authorities, and could be avoided if a new platform was provided on the northern side of the triangle, and preferably two. As the busiest commuter station left between Leeds and Bradford, Shipley was, therefore, ripe for development. The various stages in the alterations made at this important junction station are also described and illustrated.

Transferring from the major to the relatively minor station developments, within the West Yorkshire Metro area (zones 1–5) no less than twenty-one new stations have been added to the commuter network since 1968, plus one each inside North Yorkshire on the Skipton/Leeds, and Harrogate/Leeds routes. Moreover, these twenty-one form only about a third of the sixty-seven stations existing within zones 1–5, and hardly any of the large majority (forty-six) of these have not had a considerable refurbishment of some kind over the years. All the twenty-three new stations (twenty-one in West Yorkshire and two in North Yorkshire) are, however, unstaffed; two have only one platform, the rest have two, and with only five exceptions, all have regular *direct* services to either Leeds, Bradford or both. These are all subsequently listed chronologically along with information on further new stations soon to be added to the list, plus others that are only currently proposals.

The developments outlined in this book relate almost solely to the passenger services and hardly consider freight traffic. In contrast to previous eras, today very few freight movements originate within the Metro area, though many long-distance workings pass through, just a few of which appear here.

The timetabled train services run by the various Train Operating Companies are deliberately not subject to scrutiny either. These are inevitably overhauled from time to time as demand dictates, new stations open or Regional electrification schemes are implemented.

It will also be noted that the photographic captions do not dwell unduly on the detail of the locomotive, or type of stock, preferring a more general description.

Before embarking on the main chapters, it is perhaps instructive to remind ourselves of the fifty-four stations that were victims of the Beeching axe, and the sixteen others that were named for closure but escaped. The number of these closed stations that have been subsequently reopened is quite surprising, and is indicative of the resurgence of rail travel – especially commuter traffic – in the ensuing years. Although this process is most marked in West Yorkshire, neighbouring Authorities have been adding new stations to their networks as well (ten in South Yorkshire and four in North Yorkshire) in the same period, and this trend looks likely to continue.

Stations Closed (or Proposed for Closure) as a result of the Beeching Report, on lines that are (or were) within the current Metro Network

LEEDS/BRADFORD/AIREDALE/WHARFEDALE LINES

Armley Canal Road	Leeds (Central) (29.04.67)
Kirkstall	Armley Moor (04.07.66)
Newlay & Horsforth	Bramley (04.07.66)
Calverley & Rodley	Stanningley (01.01.68)
Apperley Bridge & Rawdon	Laisterdyke (04.07.66)
Saltaire	Pudsey Greenside (15.06.64)
Steeton & Silsden	Pudsey Lowtown (15.06.64)
Kildwick & Crosshills	
Cononley	The following were Proposed, but closure was not implemented;
Manningham	Ilkley
Frizinghall	Ben Rhydding
Addingham	Burley-in-Wharfedale
Otley	Menston
Pool-in-Wharfedale	Guiseley
Arthington	

(all the left-hand column closed on 22.03.65)

LEEDS/WETHERBY/HARROGATE (Line closed on 06.01.64)

Penda's Way	Scholes
Thorner	Bardsey
Collingham Bridge	Wetherby
Thorp Arch	

CALDER VALLEY and branches

Low Moor	Cleckheaton
Lightcliffe	Liversedge
Heckmondwike	Northorpe (North Road)

(these six closed 14.06.65)
plus Brighouse (05.01.70)

WAKEFIELD LINE

Ardsley (04.07.66)	Proposed but not implemented;
Fitzwilliam (06.11.67)	South Elmsall
Hemsworth (06.11.67)	

PONTEFRACT LINE

Castleford (Cutsyke)
Pontefract (Tanshelf)
Featherstone (all closed 02.01.67)

Proposed but not implemented;
Pontefract (Monkhill)
Knottingley

HUDDERSFIELD LINE

Longwood & Milnsbridge
Slaithwaite
Golcar (all three closed 07.10.68)

Proposed but not implemented;
Marsden

PENISTONE LINE

Berry Brow (04.07.66)
Skelmanthorpe (24.01.83)
Clayton West (24.01.83)

Proposed but not implemented;

Lockwood	Honley
Brockholes	Stocksmoor
Shepley	Denby Dale

OTHER STATIONS

Dewsbury (Central) (07.09.64)
Horbury & Ossett (05.01.70)
Haigh (13.09.65)

Ossett (07.09.64)
Crigglestone (13.09.65)
Altofts (12.05.90 – eventually!)
Proposed but not implemented;
Woodlesford

Chapter One

Bradford

OLD EXCHANGE becomes NEW INTERCHANGE

The pre-1968 Legacy

The line between Bradford and Leeds (via Bramley) was, at 9½ miles, considerably shorter than the 13½ mile Airedale route, but also considerably more difficult to operate. The first 2 miles from Exchange to Laisterdyke was mostly at 1 in 50 (right from the platform end), and the exit from Leeds to Armley Moor was similarly graded for part of the way, though Beeching closures had accounted for all the intermediate stations except the recently built New Pudsey (opened 6 March 1967). Despite the hilly terrain, it was this route that now ran all the Bradford/Leeds d.m.u. services after 1965; local trains to Wakefield had been axed by 1966, as had the remaining stations to Halifax in 1965 – both being Beeching cuts. However, ten through trains per day were despatched from Exchange to King's Cross (all running via Leeds and reversing direction there); indeed the last steam hauled passenger train to Leeds was the Bradford portion of a King's Cross service on 1 October 1967. *The Devonian* and *The Cornishman* still ended their journeys here from Paignton and Penzance respectively, again after reversal in Leeds, and all these expresses were loco-hauled. On the other hand, Exchange's bread-and-butter trains were the Calder Valley diesel multiple units running between Liverpool/Manchester and Leeds/York, operating on an hourly frequency each way for much of the day, though as Exchange was a terminal station these all changed direction here.

The split between the Halifax and Leeds routes occurred about ½ mile south of Exchange, with the Calder Valley line going straight on (due south) whilst the line to Leeds turned sharply to the east, both lines climbing steeply.

Exchange station itself boasted ten platforms, a relic from Lancashire & Yorkshire (L&Y) and Great Northern Railway (GNR) days when each Company effectively had half each, and the name 'Exchange' dated from 1867. A century later covered platform provision was in short supply as much of the glass in the overall roof at the south end was noticeable by its absence. The main public entrance, which was on the north-west side of the station, brought pedestrians, taxis and mail vans onto the concourse, and two flights of steps down to local thoroughfares were the only other means of access to the concourse where all the passenger facilities were grouped; car parking space was wherever you could find it on the street!

Post-1968 Developments

The station infrastructure had not been modernised for many years – probably since the 1880s – and because of this Exchange was looking run-down, and the state of the overall roof was causing some concern. Traffic levels were such that the building itself was clearly too large for the services on offer, and all its facilities were in dire need of upgrading, and this included the large road bridge spanning all the tracks at the south end of the platforms. Appropriately therefore, it was here that the first major station redevelopment began in 1972, when a start was made on the demolition of the old ten-platform Exchange, having decided that, long term, the sensible option was to remove the road overbridge completely, support the road on an embankment and replace the old station by constructing a new four-platform version a few yards to the south of the road.

When the large Bridge Street Goods Depot immediately south of the passenger terminus had been closed in 1962, a large area of land became available and Bradford Corporation drew up a long-term plan whereby a rebuilt railway station and an extensive bus and coach station could operate jointly on this site as a central transport interchange for the city. This scheme was eventually approved and work began on its first phase, demolishing Exchange and constructing its replacement, in February 1972. This new station would have to be built slightly to one side of the existing tracks, to enable timetabled services to continue to operate from the original station until the new platforms became available. Progress was sufficiently advanced on the new station for BR to close the old Exchange on 13 January 1973, trains thereafter running from two long platforms of the new, smaller terminus. By June the new station had two long and two short platforms in operation, with the short platforms situated to the east of the long ones, all four being at a higher level than Exchange's originals. Colour-light signals had also been installed to replace the semaphores, and Mill Lane signal box was updated to control these. Meanwhile the buildings of the old station were demolished and the site cleared for temporary use as a car park prior to the area becoming the permanent home for new Law Courts.

In 1974 the WYPTE began to coordinate rail and road services within the conurbation, and by 1977 the bus and coach station, built alongside the new railway station (with a common entrance to both) was ready for a joint opening ceremony as the Metro Travel Interchange on 27 March. Interestingly this was preceded on 19 March by an Open Day which featured Western Region HST 253 021 on display, a year before the Eastern Region gained its own allocation of Class 254 HSTs. (The rail station was still called Exchange at this time; it was to be 1983 before it was officially renamed Interchange in the timetable.) The Bridge Street communal entrance to the Interchange, with taxi rank and short-stay car park immediately outside, plus nearby long-stay and multi-storey car parks, is again at the north-west end of the station, though there is an additional pedestrian entrance a little further up Bridge Street as well. The main entrance opens out onto a central concourse, with escalators and steps ascending to the railway platforms from the left side of the concourse, and to the bus station from the right. There is no level connection between the rail and road sections, all transfers requiring the use of the up/down escalators/steps (a major flaw in the original concept, in the author's opinion). Consequent upon bus deregulation in 1986 (when transport integration went out and the 'benefits' of competition came in) the bus station was partly demolished in 1999, rebuilt and reopened in smaller form in 2001, though on the same site.

Due to intervention by the WYPTE (under Section 20 of the 1968 Transport Act) local rail services began to be supported financially in 1976. This brought improved timetable frequencies and the hope that, at last, the future of local rail services in West Yorkshire was going to be secure. The following table, giving changes in numbers of passengers 1977–1980, gives some measure of the early success along the Bradford– Leeds corridor and the Airedale and Wharfedale commuter lines for this period.

	1977	1980	Change
Leeds–Keighley	506,000	598,000	+18.18%
Bradford–Keighley	103,000	218,000	+111.65%
Bradford–Ilkley	645,000	944,000	+46.35%
Leeds–Bradford	1,169,000	1,452,000	+24.2%

Though only one of the above routes served Exchange directly, these lines all showed healthy growth and justified further WYPTE (and local council) funding into the 1980s.

Hammerton Street Diesel Maintenance Depot, just short of Laisterdyke, which had been the first in England to receive an allocation of d.m.u.s in 1954, closed on 13 May 1984 and the various goods yards scattered around Bradford fared no better, all but one disappearing during the 1980s. The only remaining originating traffic is the flow of scrap-metal trains from European Metal Recycling at Laisterdyke through to Liverpool Docks, running 'as required'. This interesting working drops down into Interchange in order for the diesel loco to run round the wagons (in platform 1); it is most unusual for a freight service to do this in a passenger terminal. The train then heads off to Leeds (Neville Hill up siding), where it reverses again before heading west, thus also becoming one of the few freights to pass through Leeds station on a regular (though infrequent) basis.

One item of good news for the Bradford/ Leeds services was the opening of a new station at Bramley on 12 September 1983 – on the site of the old one closed in 1965, though now with staggered platforms, and of course unstaffed.

With electrification reaching Leeds in 1988, BR announced that from October the two remaining through London trains (down from ten in 1968!) – one to King's Cross and one to St Pancras – would run to and from Bradford (Forster Square) instead of Interchange, and serve Shipley *en route*. (This reversed the 1967 switch whereby Forster Square lost its Inter-City trains to Exchange.) At this time the Airedale route was not yet electrified, and the full-length King's Cross train had to be dragged (complete with electric loco) for the last 13½ miles to and from Leeds by a diesel loco, or use HST units throughout.

Steam specials have always been thin on the ground in Bradford, but one did appear at Interchange on January 21 2006 – probably for the first time in preservation days – when 'Black Five' 45407 took out the 'Bradford Residential' to Manchester Victoria and return, a real throwback to earlier times. (Other steam specials visiting Bradford before heading for the scenic Settle & Carlisle line had, of course, to leave from Forster Square.) Still in 2006 – just – on 23 December an interesting special working of the 'Northern Belle' set from Halifax to Harrogate brought Class 67s 67001/016 top-and-tailing the stock in and out of Interchange, rare indeed to see a loco-hauled train here, even though these were diesels!

With respect to Interchange station itself, little significant structural improvement has been seen in recent years. A modest facelift took place in 2008 and the track layout was altered so that trains from both the Leeds and Halifax directions could approach the station at the same time. The severe speed restriction over this final approach was also raised slightly. In 2009 the information displays were replaced, and automatic ticket barriers were installed in 2010. Also in that year Interchange regained a through service to London when open access operator Grand Central began operating via Halifax, Pontefract and Doncaster to King's Cross with their Class 180 diesel units, which commenced running on 23 May 2010; three return workings at first, four from December 2013. These trains are therefore unusual in Interchange nowadays in the sense that they both start from and terminate at Bradford. The vast majority of services simply reverse at Interchange on their way east towards Leeds, or west towards Halifax and Manchester.

Passenger usage of Interchange has, in the last ten years (2005–2014), increased by about 25 per cent to just on 3 million per year judged by tickets bought from, or terminating at this station. It is also worth noting that there are plans to open a new station at Low Moor

(3 miles south of Interchange on the Halifax line) where the original station was closed in 1965, and these plans should come to fruition in May 2017. Further possible developments are the introduction of services to Liverpool (Lime Street), to Manchester Airport and perhaps to Chester, as part of Network Rail's 'Northern Hub' scheme, but these proposals are as yet undated, especially as this scheme was 'on hold' for several months before being reinstated again.

Principal entrance to Exchange station was via Drake Street (off Bridge Street). Note the yellow *Telegraph & Argus* newspaper delivery vans on the left. (*25 August 1972*)

Part of the old Bradford Exchange concourse with step-access to the adjacent thoroughfares Drake Street and Leeds Road at a lower level. Note the North Eastern Region tangerine signage. (*17 August 1972*)

Having just terminated in platform 7, a Calder Valley d.m.u. stands next to Leeds-bound Met-Cam unit in platform 8. (*17 July 1972*)

The 11.50 to King's Cross departs beneath semaphore signals, whilst the beginnings of the new station platforms take shape, at a slightly higher level than the old station. (*25 August 1972*)

In the early days of the adjacent bus station construction, a clear view was obtainable of platform 1, into which train 1L09 (next photo) was running. (*14 January 1973*)

Through train from King's Cross arrives in the new platform 1 at Bradford Exchange (with run-round loop line on the right). Semaphore signals have now been removed, but not the gantry; new track laid in platform 2, but not yet taken up from Exchange's old exit. (*14 January 1973*)

During the new-build phase, remaining platforms at the old station were used for stabling empty coaching stock. (*14 January 1973*)

Demolition of the Bridge Street lattice-girder bridge in front of the old station, now denuded of all track. (*17 February 1973*)

The short platforms 3 & 4 in the process of construction at the new Exchange. The shell of the former overall roof remains, though the lattice-girder road bridge has been demolished. The Victoria Hotel dominates the background. (*26 April 1973*)

With the adjacent bus/coach station yet to obscure the view, for a while vistas across central Bradford opened up – right through to the Alhambra (below the platform sign); even a Bradford Corporation bus can be seen distantly as a Blackpool train awaits departure. (*2 August 1974*)

The exit from Exchange was severe, both in terms of gradient and curvature. Here King's Cross train 1A21 rounds the curve at St Dunstans heading for Leeds. Blackpool trains, heading for Halifax, would go straight on past the new building on the left. (*15 June 1974*)

Empty stock for 1A21 arrives in platform 2. Note the recently stone-cleaned retaining wall, and colour-light signals installed. (*3 May 1975*)

In addition to the run-round loop at platform 1, it was also possible to run round in platform 2, though this pointwork has long since been removed. (*3 May 1975*) Two days later an additional 35 trains per day swelled the Leeds/Bradford timetable. See 'tickets' in the appendix.

After using the engine release points at the buffer stops and running round, the Brush type 2 lifts train 1A21 up the 1 in 50 to St Dunstans, a stiff task for these moderately powered diesels. (*25 October 1974*)

Once the replacement station was complete, services returned to normal. Calder Valley sets ran the Manchester/Blackpool/Leeds trains (on the left) and other first generation d.m.u.s ran the shorter services. London expresses continued to use locomotive-hauled coaching stock. (*2 August 1975*)

Building of the new bus/coach station is now well advanced, whilst an empty Exchange station basks in sunshine. (*February 1976*)

Many years later, structurally very little has changed. The retaining wall is no longer pristine, but the Class 15x series multiple units look smart in their Northern franchise livery. They are, however, approaching 30 years old, with no immediate sign of replacement. (*6 August 2015*)

Virtually all local/regional services are in the hands of Northern's Sprinter or Pacer units; here a 2-car Class 150 Sprinter heads for Leeds. (*6 August 2015*)

A 4-car set consisting of two 2-car Class 142 Pacers comes gingerly down the hill from St Dunstans curve, ex-Leeds. (*6 August 2015*)

After a gap of several years, a direct service to King's Cross was provided by Grand Central trains from 2010. The route is not exactly 'direct' however, and generally takes 3 to 3½ hours, compared to just over 2 hours from Leeds via Virgin trains. Here the empty stock of the 17.54 arrival (14.48 from London) heads off to Crofton depot. (*6 August 2015*)

This is the main, joint, entrance off Bridge Street into Bradford Interchange. The railway platforms are beyond the double-decker bus turning into the bus station. Drake Street did, of course, lead to the old Exchange's main entrance. (*13 September 2006*)

Chapter Two

Bradford

OLD FORSTER SQUARE becomes NEW FORSTER SQUARE

The pre-1968 Legacy

This Midland Railway station of 1890 had been modernised in the mid-1950s; a new concourse had been provided, the overall roof had been demolished and the six terminal platforms covered by awnings of contemporary design. There was capacity a-plenty here when the mid-1960s closures took away the Leeds local services completely, and the Inter-City trains to St Pancras and to the West Country were transferred across to Exchange station in 1967. Henceforward a sparse service of 2-car d.m.u.s running to and from Keighley, and up the Wharfedale line as far as Ilkley, were the only remaining passenger services left operating, and these required very little platform space.

Post-1968 Developments

What did need substantial platform space was the considerable volume of parcels traffic emanating from the Bradford mail-order firms of Gratton and Empire Stores. This traffic was buoyant throughout the 1960s, and into the 1970s, until these firms gradually switched to road deliveries, and other discount stores ate into the local firm's market. When BR finally closed its Collection & Delivery parcels service in 1980, Forster Square was largely desolate, with only platform 2 and the short platform 1 in regular use. Some of the carriage sidings (and also the empty platforms) did see occasional usage in the 1980s as storage space for withdrawn

Great Eastern line electric units prior to their scrapping.

Upon local government reorganisation in 1972, Bradford Corporation became the City of Bradford Metropolitan District Council, and in conjunction with other newly-formed Metropolitan areas – Leeds, Calderdale (Halifax), Kirklees (Huddersfield) and Wakefield – decided to support local bus and train services financially from 1976 onwards. Under the auspices of the West Yorkshire Passenger Transport Executive (WYPTE), this subsidisation began to transform the remaining rail routes to the extent that enhanced Keighley/Bradford services were, a few years later, also calling at new stations at Crossflatts (opened in 1982), Saltaire (reopened in 1984) and, closest to Forster Square, Frizinghall (re-opened in 1987). Wharfedale line stations as far as Ilkley had escaped the Beeching axe, but were joined in 1973 by the reopening of Baildon Station (between Shipley and Guiseley) on 5 January – exactly twenty years after its previous closure – with funding from Bradford and Baildon Councils.

The large ex-LMS Goods Warehouse next to Forster Square station was knocked down in 1975, and it was apparent then that further rationalisation would soon follow.

From the accompanying diagram of the rail layout close to Forster Square, it will be seen that a great deal of this space was redundant by the 1980s, and with the 1984 closure of Valley

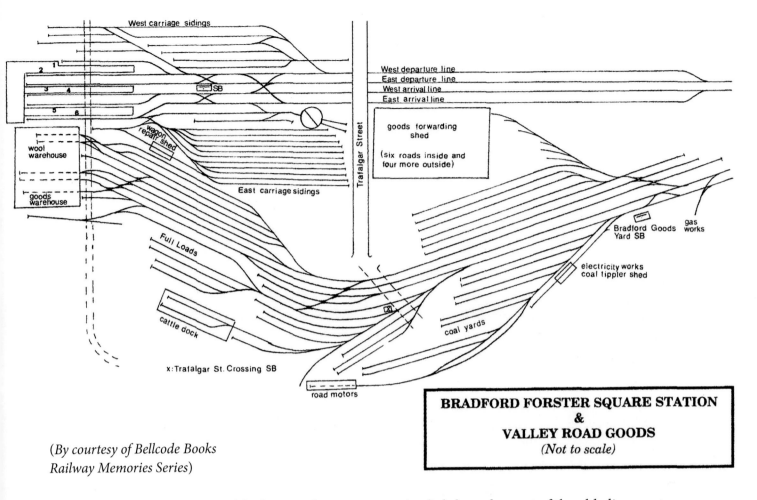

West carriage sidings

West departure line
East departure line
West arrival line
East arrival line

goods forwarding
shed

(six roads inside and
four more outside)

SB

wool
warehouse

goods
warehouse

wagon
repair shed

Trafalgar Street

East carriage sidings

Bradford Goods
Yard SB

gas
works

electricity works
coal tippler shed

Full Loads

cattle dock

coal yards

x:Trafalgar St.Crossing SB

road motors

*(By courtesy of Bellcode Books
Railway Memories Series)*

**BRADFORD FORSTER SQUARE STATION
&
VALLEY ROAD GOODS**
(Not to scale)

Road Goods Yard and Depot (the last goods yard in Bradford), much land became available for redevelopment which, if the area taken up by most of the underused station could be added, would be a prime commercial prospect. Such large schemes tend to have a long gestation period however, and additionally the first plans also fell through, causing further delay to any commercial development.

Also in 1984, with so few timetabled train movements in and out of the terminus, the signal box was closed and control exercised from the Bradford Junction 'box at Shipley (via colour lights of course). A number of steam specials bound for the classic Settle & Carlisle route did, however, grace the terminus around this time, and for a few years afterwards.

What was not delayed was approval of the plans for the replacement station. This would be a couple of hundred yards north of the original, and again slightly to the west of the old alignment, so that remaining services could run uninterrupted whilst building the new and demolishing the old stations commenced in parallel, in 1989/90. Rapid progress was, therefore, made in constructing this 3-platform station, with one short platform and a long island platform designed to accommodate full-length Inter-City trains. Interestingly, although pedestrian access is still possible from Forster Square itself (via the bottom of Cheapside), a substantial new pedestrian entrance consisting of a lift and stairs complex has been installed at the end of School Street (at the top of Cheapside) where there is a considerable height difference from this new western entrance down to the valley floor where the station is situated. The main entrance and vehicular forecourt is, however, reached from Valley Road on the eastern side of the new station, still named Forster Square, after the Bradford MP W.E. Forster – he of the

1870 Education Act. The new, smaller version of Forster Square finally opened in 1990, and after demolition of the remains of the old station and site clearance, part of the vacant space was used as a car park before another commercial development plan finally received authority to proceed.

Therefore, when BR announced that (as from October 1988) the two remaining trains from London to Interchange would be transferred to run into Forster Square, no move had yet been made to transform the large derelict 'redevelopment' area directly opposite that would welcome these expresses – not a very positive advertisement for Bradford! (Leeds at this time enjoyed fifteen through trains each way!). Nowadays the view from all trains is utterly dominated by the rear of the adjacent commercial retail park and this is not a happy alternative either!

The new station opened in 1990 and was electrified in early 1995, along with the Airedale line to Skipton & Leeds, and the Wharfedale line to Ilkley, and the obliteration of the former station is nowadays almost complete. A little of the original Midland Railway's curtain wall facing the station's main entrance of 1890 and fronting Forster Square remains, as a reminder that once upon a long time ago, Bradford was sufficiently important for Britain's first Pullman train service to depart from here to St Pancras in 1874! A plaque to commemorate this event has been prominently installed by the Pullman Society within the new station complex.

Currently, 4-car Class 333 e.m.u.s (with occasional variations) operate all the local services to Skipton, Ilkley and Leeds, and a Class 91 electric loco, hauling Mk 4 stock, forms the sole Monday to Saturday early morning King's Cross-bound departure, with reversal at Leeds. Passenger numbers using Forster Square over the ten-year period 2004/05 to 2013/14 have amazingly quintupled to a shade over 2 million per year, so someone must be doing something right!

A slightly early shot as this scene is dated February 1967! It does, however, give such an excellent overall view of the extent of the infrastructure beyond the platform end at Forster Square – coach sidings on the left, with the extensive Valley Road Goods Depot, beyond the incoming 'Harrogate Sunday Pullman' (diverted from Exchange), to the right. All this was to disappear; even the buildings on Valley Road itself! (*February 1967; Colour-Rail.com*)

Panning to the right of the previous shot reveals a busy 6-platform station abounding with traffic (especially parcels) and dominated by the huge Midland Railway Goods & Wool Warehouse. All of this will also be demolished. (*May 1971; Colour-Rail.com*)

Demolition began with the Warehouse mentioned above; a view looking north over the station with Bradford City's floodlights prominent on the left horizon. (*15 March 1975*)

A better view of the internal capacity that this large, but now redundant, warehouse once possessed. (*15 March 1975*)

The 2E73 was a summer Saturday Morecambe/Leeds working that ran into Forster Square and reversed there before stopping at Shipley on its way eastwards. Seen here on 16 August 1975, arriving in platform 6.

Flying Scotsman in Bradford! Seen at the head of the empty stock of the 'North Yorkshireman' excursion train in platform 4. (See also Keighley, Airedale Line section) (*23 June 1981*)

More steam in Forster Square! This time it's 34092 *City of Wells*, an engine based on the Worth Valley Railway and heading a special excursion to Keighley. (*9 June 1985*)

A much sadder sight. Valley Road Goods Depot now abandoned and lifted, and track only remaining into platforms 1 & 2, which is where the 12.40 SuO Forster Square/St Pancras HST can be seen across the dereliction in the foreground. (*23 October 1988*)

The contrast between the occupants of platform 2 could hardly be greater, as a 2-car Class 144 Pacer requires minimal space on a local service. (*10 March 1990*)

Bradford Forster Square; two tracks still run into the old platforms 1 & 2, whilst the new, long, island platform (to become numbers 1 & 2) has yet to be finished. A new, short, platform 3 will eventually emerge from behind the right-hand vegetation. Bradford Cathedral (with flag) catches the sun. (*7 April 1990*)

New platforms 1 & 2 are still unfinished, but the 19.45 to King's Cross is about to be dragged to Leeds by a diesel locomotive before the electric engine can take over on reversal at Leeds. Electrification of the Aire Valley route is still nearly five years away! (*July 1990*)

The new Forster Square is now fully functioning, and the yellow crane in the background is helping to install the high-level access on the west side of the station. All six old trackless platforms are in evidence – but not for long – as a 3-car Class 144 Pacer takes out a local service from the new platform 3. (*30 August 1990*)

All remains of the old station are now gone. High-level access is at last complete (low level pedestrian entrance is behind this, from the bottom of Cheapside) and *Green Arrow* (with support coach) awaits the arrival of a special which it will head to Carlisle. (*23 May 1992*)

The 'Cumbrian Mountain Express' has come into platform 1 behind *Green Arrow*, which will detach here and diesel power will take over. Commercial development has yet to start on the large vacant plot next to the new station. (*1 August 1992*)

The new inner ring-road bridge has appeared over the platform ends, though not yet open for traffic. The space on the left was designated a public area; unfinished here, it has since become an untended jungle, sadly. Local trains are in the hands of, typically, Class 144 3-car units. (*April 1993*)

The new high-level entrance halfway up Cheapside proclaims itself at the (shortened) end of School Street. (*April 1993*)

The strictly functional lift & stairs structure is now seen from ground level, subsequent developments will obscure this view completely. The main, vehicular, entrance will appear in due course behind the brick-coloured builder's storage block. (*April 1993*)

Passengers gazing at the vacant space in front of them have, for a time, a clear view across to the retaining wall of the old warehouse and the abutment that supported the continuation of School Street. (*April 1993*)

A few months later, 46229 *Duchess of Hamilton* would temporarily block the view, with an enthusiasts' special from Carlisle. (*5 August 1993*)

This time *Duke of Gloucester* waits to take over an incoming special. Unfortunately the engine is positioned directly beneath Hamm Strasse (the recently opened inner ring-road) enveloping the bridge in smoke and steam. Motorists unwittingly thought the bridge was on fire and called the Fire Brigade, who closed the road to investigate! (*29 January 1994*)

In commemoration of the
First Pullman Car service in Britain

On 1st June 1874,
the first Pullman train in Great Britain
left this station for London, St Pancras

THE PULLMAN SOCIETY

Within the new station's booking hall, this plaque adorns the wall as a reminder of Bradford's rather grander status in Victorian times. 'This station' is several times removed from the original 1874 version, not in quite the same place and wasn't called Forster Square! (*13 September 2006*)

Current services are usually operated by Class 333 units but 321s fill-in from time to time. These began life by working the Doncaster route, but still look the part when freshly painted; autumn colours also help! (*23 October 2015*)

The main vehicular entrance to the station is on the eastern side, off Valley Road, and is a fairly low-key modern building, dominated by the stone cladding enclosing the lift and stairs from the high-level entrance on School Street. (*6 July 2016*)

Class 333 units (already 15 years old!) are now the regular form of transport. Unrestricted growth of vegetation is denying passengers the view of 'Mothercare's back door, part of the huge retail park that now totally dominates the 3-platform station. (*25 October 2015*)

Chapter Three

Shipley

CHANGES WITH THE TIMES and FOR THE TIMES

The pre-1968 Legacy

Shipley is a staffed junction station 2¾ miles north of Bradford Forster Square and 10¾ miles west of Leeds City. At the beginning of 1968 the station had four platforms on two sides of a curved triangular layout, with no platforms on the Leeds/ Skipton direct line (the third side of the triangle or 'north curve').

Platforms 1 & 2: formed the north-west curve and dealt with the Forster Square/Keighley trains (platform 1) and trains from Keighley to Bradford on platform 2.

This was an infrequent d.m.u. service of 10-12 trains per day.

Platforms 3 & 4: formed the north-east curve and dealt with the Wharfedale line traffic between Forster Square and Ilkley; to Ilkley on platform 3, from Ilkley on platform 4.

This was roughly an hourly d.m.u. service, with extras in the rush hours.

These basic services were supplemented by some Leeds/Skipton trains and Leeds/Morecambe services, as outlined below. Additional trains also passed through; parcels trains mostly to and from Forster Square, freight traffic and Leeds/Carlisle expresses that ran round the north curve.

Three stepless ramps connected all four platforms from a subway running beneath all the tracks at the Bradford end of the station. The main vehicular access was via an unnamed cobbled approach road from the north, passing under the north curve, directly to the Booking Hall. This was situated at the southern apex of the triangle where platforms 2 and 3 merge, at the top of the central ramp from the subway. From Station Road (*cul-de-sac*) – parallel to platform 1 – passengers could walk, or park on this street, and then enter directly onto platform 1 or go via the ramps and subway to the Booking Hall. (The subway continued beyond platform 4 beneath the two goods lines that bypassed the station towards Bradford, and exited onto a path though this exit/ entrance was later closed off.)

After 22 March 1965, when all seven intermediate stations were closed, Shipley became the only open station between Forster Square and Leeds. At that time all Bradford/Leeds services were transferred to run from Exchange into Central, until the closure of Central on 29 April 1967, and subsequently into City. As soon as the rebuilt Leeds City station opened on 1 May 1967, through trains from Forster Square to St Pancras, and to the West Country, were diverted to run from Exchange, so Shipley lost its Inter-City trains as well.

From March 1965 passengers travelling from Leeds to Shipley were served by some of the Leeds/Skipton d.m.u. trains running into platform 4, stopping and then going forward to beyond Bradford Junction signal box before reversing and proceeding into platform 1, stopping again for any Skipton-bound business and for the driver to change ends, before setting off again. In the reverse direction, Leeds-bound trains ran into platform 2 stopped, drew forward, reversed into platform 3, stopped again (extra traffic plus driver changing ends) and then headed for Leeds. This was cumbersome to say the least! It was simplified to some extent after April 1966 when Leeds/Skipton trains simply ran round the north curve past Bingley Junction signal box, and then reversed in and out of platform 1. In addition to which, passengers from Bradford to Skipton and *vice versa* were obliged to change trains at Keighley onto the Leeds/Skipton service. (The author recalls a morning commuter journey into Leeds when the driver, having switched ends in platform 3, found the main control column to be inoperable. Solution; drive from the rear cab with the guard relaying the signal aspects from the front cab to the driver! On another occasion a power failure at Leeds station caused passengers to officially de-train onto the tracks (if at Whitehall Junction or closer) or in the author's case, onto the defunct Holbeck (Low Level) platform from where we were led down to the main road through the (specially unlocked) iron gates.)

Loco-hauled trains such as those from Leeds to Morecambe, ran past Bingley Junction box and reversed in and out of platform 1 before continuing west. East-bound trains ran into platform 2 and then reversed back out again past Bingley Junction before heading to Leeds via the north curve.

Post-1968 Developments

It is apparent from the above description that the 'in & out' method of working the local services at Shipley was a retrograde step, and would ultimately lead to the provision of a platform (no.5) on the north curve, though this would not be achieved (for Skipton-bound trains) until 14 May 1979! Earlier, during 1978 and prior to platform 5 being constructed, the three engineers sidings within the triangle were taken up and the area tarmacked to provide free car parking space (which quickly filled on a daily basis!).

With only one platform (no.5) put in (on the down side), up trains (to Leeds) still had to run 'wrong line' between cross-overs placed some distance on either side of this extra platform, which was accessed by means of a new footpath direct from the Booking Hall and straight across the car park. It was, however, to be a further year (9 March 1980) before the cross-overs were installed and ready for use by up trains. In the meantime these had to continue running into platform 2 and reversing back out again and then proceeding towards Leeds. This development was clearly only a 'halfway house' measure, with the obvious solution of building a second platform on the outside of the curve not being brought to fruition until 25 July 1992!

(When platform 5 was opened, Shipley became one of only two stations in the entire UK to operate timetabled services on all three sides of a triangular layout, the only other currently being Earlestown. Historically such stations were always rare, and have only ever previously totalled five: Queensbury, Ambergate, Rutherglen, Forres, Earlestown and now Shipley. The first four have either closed completely or lost services on at least one side, Shipley being the only one to have joined the list rather than being deleted from it.)

A further alteration to the infrastructure once platform 5 had been opened and bi-directionally signalled, was to take platform 1 out of use on 30 March 1980, and remove the track from there as this platform had the tightest curvature. Two-way working was then introduced on platform 2 so that the Bradford/Keighley service could use this platform in both directions.

Meanwhile, out of passengers' gaze, further closures and track rationalisation were taking place. The remaining Idle/Shipley (Windhill) freight stub (with goods traffic formerly running from Laisterdyke as far as Skipton and to Bradford Valley Road) was closed on 5 October 1968 and taken out of use on 22 June 1969 – the same date as the goods lines into Bradford behind platform 4 were officially closed. All these rails were lifted soon after their closure. The 4-track section between Thackley Tunnel and Shipley was reduced, in stages, to two tracks and the Ilkley line was singled through to Guiseley, both from the Shipley and from the Leeds directions.

The station itself underwent significant modifications. In 1968 all four platforms still had (either in whole or in part) their 1885 Midland Railway canopies, originally all about 300 ft long but over the years these had been partially taken down, to no obvious pattern. Platform 1, once closed, was largely dismantled (along with its redundant buildings) leaving only a short section (plus canopy) at the subway entrance, whilst in 1973/4 platforms 3 & 4 were reduced in length at the north end, to 300 ft only, and some buildings closed or removed. At this time the remaining lengths of canopy also disappeared (except for a short section on platform 4 at the top of the subway) though all buildings and retaining walls were beautifully stone-cleaned! Gas-lighting was also removed and replaced (at long last!) with electric lights. In 1980 platform 2 was also effectively shortened, as, in the absence of platform 1, the single track from Bingley Junction had been slewed away from the north end, which was then prohibited to passengers. However, perhaps surprisingly, in October 1988

the remaining King's Cross/Bradford expresses were diverted away from Bradford Interchange to Forster Square, with stops at Shipley in each direction. If these services were operated by HST units this wasn't a problem, but electrically-hauled trains had to be dragged to Bradford by a diesel loco! To cope better with these London expresses, platform 3 was made bi-directional from 25 September 1988, but it was only on 14 May 1990 that this platform was extended to 790 ft to accommodate a full-length Inter-City train. (Platform 4 was not altered again. When built, platform 1 had been the longest at 650 ft, all others 550 ft.)

As mentioned earlier, the long-awaited second platform on the north curve was finally brought into use on 25 July 1992. This was not, however, to be designated no.6!

At this time, since no.1 had not existed for a dozen years, a rethink produced the (now current) system, whereby the numbering is as follows:

Platform 1	(north curve) up trains, Skipton/Leeds.
Platform 2	(north curve) down trains, Leeds/Skipton.
Platform 3	(bi-directional) Bradford/Leeds and Bradford/Ilkley.
Platform 4	Leeds or Ilkley/Bradford.
Platform 5	(bi-directional) Bradford/Skipton and v.v.

The 1979 platform on the north curve (now platform 2) was accessed by a footpath directly from the Booking Hall, and when this was joined by the new platform 1 a footbridge was installed at the Bingley Junction end to connect the two. A level pedestrian access off the adjoining street was also made available, which opened straight onto platform 1 at the bottom of the footbridge stairs. At the Leeds end of platform 1 new steps also connected this platform to the vehicular approach road (built in 1885 and still cobbled!) that leads straight to the main station buildings situated in the fork of platforms 3 & 5 (new numbering). Both 'north curve' platforms, when built, were provided with only rudimentary 'bus shelters'. These have since been replaced by substantial, good-quality stone-faced waiting rooms with seating, well lit and well used, especially in winter.

The biggest change was yet to come however. Consequent upon the electrification of the East Coast Main Line as far as Leeds in 1988, plans were formulated to extend the wiring to the Airedale and Wharfedale lines, where commuter traffic had increased considerably throughout the 1980s. Both these projects were successfully completed, energised in 1994, with electric services using the 25kV AC overhead system on both lines coming on stream during 1995. The Wharfedale line terminates at Ilkley (the onward section through Addingham to Skipton closing in 1965) and the four intermediate stations on the branch itself had remained open. Ilkley services from both Leeds and Bradford Forster Square were electrified and the Bradford trains now called additionally at Baildon (reopened in 1973) and Frizinghall (reopened in 1987).

(As it was the WYPTE instigating these schemes, they had a problem with the Airedale line in as much as Skipton was in North Yorkshire, not West Yorkshire, but only at Skipton was there sufficient space to expand the storage facility and to maintain the electric stock. (It was also true that more traffic would be generated for the railway if electrification terminated at Skipton than at, say, Keighley.) However, a quick glance at the West Yorkshire Metro Map at the beginning of Chapter 5 reveals that cheap fares subsidised

by the WYPTE are not available beyond Steeton & Silsden (which reopened in May 1990), though this had not prevented Cononley – also in North Yorkshire – from reopening in April 1988. To cater for increased commuter levels on the Airedale line, Crossflatts and Saltaire had already reopened in 1982 and 1984 respectively.)

At Shipley, the infrastructure for overhead wiring changed the scene dramatically. Additionally all three manual signal boxes were closed and removed, and multiple aspect colour light signals erected instead of semaphores – a thoroughly modern railway at last! Except that, in time honoured practice, new rolling stock was not provided, and pre-used (i.e. old!) e.m.u.s were cascaded from the Great Eastern lines around London. These had already seen 30+ years of service and were high-density slam-door 3-car stock of Class 308. Happily, brand-new units of Class 333 were eventually delivered (five years later, from 2000) though again there was disappointment on their arrival in that, as built, these too were only 3-car sets which led to immediate overcrowding in the peak hours, despite an increased frequency of service. Soon strengthened to 4-car sets, these are still overcrowded in peak hours! These units now operate virtually all the local commuter services. Once the Leeds/ Bradford route via Shipley had been energised, the sole remaining through Forster Square/King's Cross train no longer required to be dragged by a diesel! However, the daily through train to King's Cross from Skipton was to remain an HST diesel unit all the way, as there was not sufficient 'juice' along Airedale to power a Class 91 and Mk4 stock! (There now is, but it's still an HST on Saturdays.)

After all the developments outlined above, it may be thought that Shipley was 'complete' and that no further work was necessary. Wrong!

Regulations regarding accessibility now demand step-free access in almost all circumstances and the footbridge between platforms 1 & 2 fell foul of this requirement. Here two lifts now connect platform level with footbridge level, and despite the fact that the subway linking platforms 3, 4 & 5 has step-free ramps to platform level, a new footbridge with two lifts has also been provided to connect platforms 3 & 4. (Presumably the ramps are deemed too steep by today's regulations, though the ramps have not been closed.) Having to clear the 25kV overhead wires makes this footbridge a tall structure of necessity, but it is nevertheless rather 'out-of-gauge' with respect to the original Victorian buildings on, and adjacent to, platform 3.

The Booking Hall opens directly onto this platform, and within the Hall there is an annexe into a café, with seating spilling into the Hall itself. The café is only open during the morning, but does a brisk trade. The Hall was entirely reconditioned and the ticket-issuing 'office' fully modernised as an accompaniment to electrification, and won the Ian Allan Railway Heritage Award in 1998, the plaque for which adorns the Hall.

The only aspect of railway operations that remained more or less constant over the years was the locally-generated freight. This emanated from the sidings south of the station that once served the Goods Shed. This was still in use during the 1970s, as was the coal yard a little further south. Both Goods Shed and coal yard no longer exist, but the scrap metal firm Crossley's (now Crossley-Evans) has been using the Goods Shed sidings since the 1950s, still does, and trainloads of scrap continued to be despatched regularly to Cardiff Tidal until roughly 2012. There has now been an interruption to this historic service for some years, and traffic flows have yet to be resumed.

These freights ran up the Aire Valley to Leeds, but then headed south via the Whitehall Jct./Engine Shed Jct curve.

Shipley is nowadays an extremely busy station. All lines are electrified and a ½ hourly service throughout most of the day is operated on the following routes;

Bradford/Leeds	Bradford/Ilkley
Bradford/Skipton	Leeds/Skipton

all of which call at Shipley, i.e. 16 trains an hour, plus…

Leeds/Morecambe/Carlisle	10-12 trains daily each way, plus…

2 Inter-City trains: Bradford/King's Cross, Skipton/King's Cross each way, plus… 'main line freight' over the Settle & Carlisle route to/from Leeds, numbers vary.

In comparison with the services through Shipley outlined at the beginning of this description, those just listed are as different as chalk and cheese. Much of the credit for this is due to the initiative of the WYPTE, newly formed in 1974, which has supported and encouraged all rail services, and station improvements, throughout West Yorkshire. They have, over the years, also been instrumental in replacing first generation d.m.u.s with 'Pacer' units of various classes (even owning some themselves), increasing service frequencies, introducing 'Super Sprinters' on other local lines, and ultimately electrifying the Airedale & Wharfedale routes. Of course increasing road congestion has been a factor in ever larger commuter numbers using trains, but a range of subsidised fares on offer within the Metro area has consistently sent very positive messages, and the successor body, the West Yorkshire Combined Authority, is pursuing the same course.

Perhaps surprisingly, the basic 1880s stone infrastructure of Shipley's approach road and main public building – the Booking Hall – have remained intact. The extensive stone-cleaning carried out in the 1970s, together with a generally cleaner atmosphere, have ensured the buildings retain a certain attractiveness, enhanced recently by the Bagnalls Group, who won the 'Industrial' category at the Painting & Decorating Association Awards Ceremony for their work on Shipley's ornate features!

Over the nine-year period 2004/05 to 2012/13 passenger usage of Shipley station has doubled from 0.831 million to 1.667 million per year, and shows no sign (yet) of levelling off.

Plainly Shipley's position astride four busy routes has caused more developments and alterations to be required here than at the average Metro station. However, all the (non-brand-new) stations have received some modifications over the years; it's just that Shipley, in its cramped Victorian location, has had to squeeze a quart into a pint pot – and has done so very successfully!

Back in 1970 Shipley looked much the same as it had for many years; canopies, gas lights, semaphores, worn-out paintwork and many wooden structures – all of which appear here as an Ilkley to Bradford train leaves platform 4, unusually a 5-car set. (*29 July 1970*)

The top of the subway slope between platforms 2 & 3 leads straight to the Booking Hall (to the right of the telephone box) and this scene typifies the outdated infrastructure of those smaller stations that had escaped the Beeching axe. (*29 July 1970*)

Platforms 1 & 2 still sported considerable lengths of canopy. The tight curvature of platform 1 will be noted. (*29 July 1970*)

Three years later and things have begun to change, as a shot taken from Bradford Junction signal box reveals. The canopies over platforms 2 & 3 have gone, the buildings have been stone-cleaned, platform 3 has been shortened, signalling has been simplified and the goods lines that bypassed the station on the right have been lifted. (*30 June 1973*)

A local freight heads west past the end of platform 1 powered by a Sulzer type 2 with 4-wheeled mineral wagons in tow. Note that stone-cleaning extended to the retaining walls, and the road bridge is about to receive another carriageway. (*29 September 1973*)

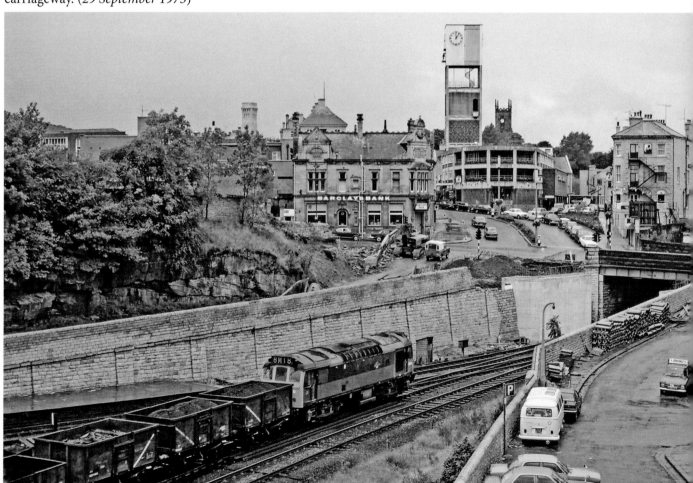

Here's a Leeds-bound train performing the in-and-out manoeuvre current at the time. Arriving at no.2, it will then draw forward past Bradford Junction 'box, reverse and pull into no.3 before departing to Leeds. Note the engineers' sidings are occupied by a selection of ballast cleaning machines and other vehicles. (*27 July 1973*)

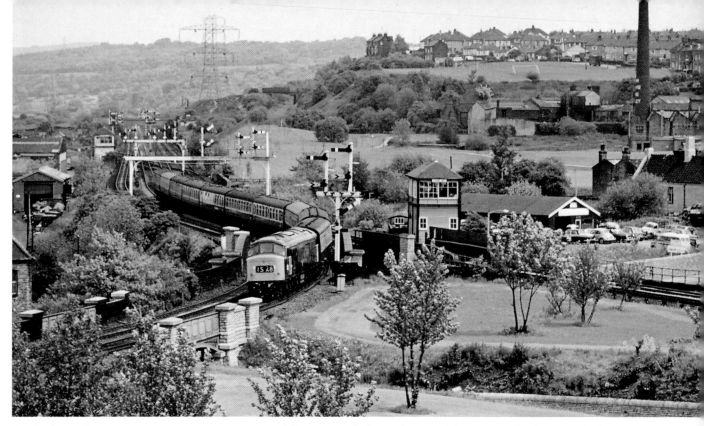

A telephoto shot gives an interesting overview of the approach from the east. The 10-coach *Thames-Clyde Express* has passed several signal gantries on the 4-track section from Thackley tunnel and is rounding the north curve of the triangle. The Ilkley line comes in behind Guiseley Junction 'box (on the left) and the building on the extreme right is the former Great Northern Railway Windhill station. The Idle branch came down the greensward behind the red 'home' signals, passing under the footbridge seen further up. (*1 June 1974*)

Meanwhile, a Bradford/Keighley local leaves a crowd of passengers on platform 1 waiting for a Leeds/Morecambe train to reverse in and take them to the seaside! (*5 August 1974*)

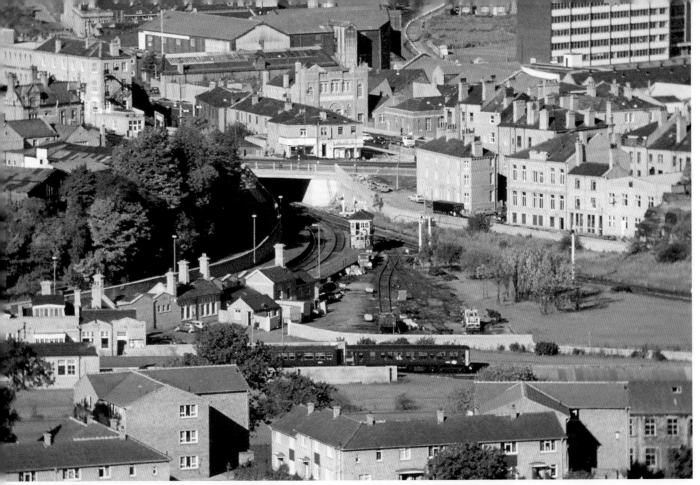

Another telephoto shot, this time of the triangle itself, looking west and revealing the extent of the stone-cleaning that took place around Shipley whilst the West Riding County Council emptied its coffers before being taken over by West Yorkshire Metropolitan Council! The Leeds/Liverpool canal can be seen at the top, and a 2-car Ilkley train is leaving from platform 3. (*6 October 1974*)

A Leeds d.m.u. awaits departure from no.3 whilst an Ilkley service comes into no.4. Significantly, semaphores have given way to colour lights controlled by Leeds Junction 'box. (*12 July 1975*)

The Morecambe/Leeds train 2E73 was described fully in the Forster Square section, and is here running into platform 2. (*2 August 1975*)

In an effort to prolong the life of aging rolling stock, a number of units were given considerable refurbishment both inside and out. The livery was changed to a brighter, cleaner appearance, and one of these sets rounds the north curve on a Leeds/Skipton service. (*1 January 1976*)

Three years later platform 5 has eventually been built and is in use, but the engineers' sidings have been removed. Windhill station (closed 1931) now sports 'Len's' on its roof. (*1 June 1979*)

Having shortened platform 3 in 1973, with the prospect of full-length London trains again stopping at Shipley, no.3 was extended to 790ft to accommodate these. At the same time, bi-directional signalling was installed so that the King's Cross train used no.3 both southbound and northbound. (*7 April 1990*)

Refurbishing old stock was only a stop-gap measure, and from the mid-1980s new Pacer units were in charge of most local services. Here a 3-car Class 144 unit departs for Keighley; platform 1 is now defunct, both the unit and the signal box bear the Metro livery and the area of the former Engineers' Sidings is now a (free) car park. (*19 May 1990*)

Platform 5 had eventually arrived in 1979, and yet the obvious platform '6' took thirteen years to come to fruition! A month prior to opening, pedestrian-access steps from the cobbled approach road (right-hand side) are unfinished. The wheelchair-friendly entrance is at the other end of the platform. (*28 June 1992*)

After this very long wait, the second platform on the north curve was finally opened in July 1992. The opportunity was also taken to renumber Shipley's platforms so that this became no.1 (not no.6) and what had been no.5 became no.2. A Leeds-bound 2-car Class 156 unit disgorges passengers; both platforms had at this time their first, rather rudimentary, shelters. (*22 August 1992*)

Nos.1 & 2 did of course receive a footbridge connection near the west end, visible here as 6201 *Princess Elizabeth* runs through platform 5 (the old no.2) with an excursion bound for the Settle & Carlisle line. (*22 August 1992*)

The new footbridge provided a good vantage point for photographs, until wiring went up! A Class 142 Pacer departs to Skipton. (*April 1993*)

The side entrance from Station Road was tidied up, and platform 5 shortened slightly at the south end. New black fencing improved the appearance further. (*April 1993*)

The last surviving stretch of original canopy covered the subway-ramp entrance to platform 4. A small loading dock, long since disused, can be seen in the foreground. (*April 1993*)

One of the useful features of a triangular layout is easy means of turning stock round. Here, *Blue Peter* had backed out of Forster Square, but by running round the triangle could return to Bradford the right way round for a later departure. Note the Goods Depot on the right, and Crossley's scrap yard beyond. (*7 August 1993*)

How freight traffic has changed over the years! 66 190 is just about in the same position as the type 2 diesel seen earlier, but taken from the opposite angle to avoid the wiring. A lengthy rake of empty hoppers trails the diesel, which is roughly three times as powerful as the one seen previously. (*30 May 2000*)

A Skipton-bound Class 308 departs from platform 5 in winter sun. These slam-door trains took a bit of getting used to after years of push-button operation on Pacers and Sprinters. (*8 February 2001*)

The one London train per day was usually hauled by a Class 91, but not always, as seen here when a Class 90 deputised on the return, late evening push towards Forster Square. (*13 September 2001*)

The rudimentary waiting shelters originally provided on platforms 1 & 2 were subsequently replaced with stone-faced waiting rooms. This is the smaller one on platform 2. (*6 June 2005*)

This is effectively a comparison shot with the second image, taken thirty-five years earlier! Note also that the Goods sheds (between the station and the scrap yard) have since been demolished. (*7 June 2005*)

Electrification of the lines had a knock-on effect on the passenger facilities, one of which was the refurbishment of Shipley's Booking Hall. This included provision of a café and various advertising displays, note the newspaper headline! (*13 September 2006*) *Inset:* The wall displays include the prestigious 1998 award, and a statement of where the money came from! (*27 April 1999*)

Although public electric services began nearly three years before, some of the building work at the station was still in progress; the subway access to platform 4 was, for instance, unfinished as a Class 308 unit heads for Bradford. (*April 1998*)

Looking down the long platform 3 towards Bradford, you would be tempted to think 'job done'. (*9 May 2007*)

Wrong! Despite the presence of subway ramps onto platforms 3 & 4, a footbridge connection (complete with lifts) was deemed necessary and was installed during 2008/9. (*30 October 2008*)

Lifts were also provided at the ends of the footbridge between the platforms on the north curve, where the 'luxury' waiting room on no.1 platform is seen to advantage. (*4 August 2015*)

Bradford's train leaves Forster Square at (06.30 SX, 07.30 SO). This is the Saturday King's Cross train, about to receive good complement of passengers on the full-length platform 3. (*8 August 2015*)

Bradford's one-per-day electric express to King's Cross is matched by a similar train from Skipton. This is seen making its early stop (07.13 on the clock tower) in platform 1, where selective door opening is necessary on such a long train as can be seen here, only 3 or 4 coaches are actually on the platform. (*5 August 2015*)

Moving away from the station itself, the following photographs look at developments immediately to the south of the platforms.

Back in 1972, Shipley Goods signal box still controlled entry to the working coal yard, as an Ilkley train heads for Bradford. The trackbed of the former goods lines is clearly visible. (*17 July 1972*)

Looking the other way from the road overbridge, Crossley's scrap yard dominates the scene, with more scrap apparently arriving. Between here and the station, Shipley's Goods depots – clearly in three sections – fill the space. (*26 April 1973*)

For a time, internal shunting within Crossley's private yard area was performed by this small 0-4-0 tank engine bearing the name *Chemicals*. (*8 March 1975*)

One of the 2-car refurbished diesel units (bearing the WYPTE symbol within the blue waistband) heads for Bradford from Ilkley. The full extent of the coal yard is seen in the background. (*5 July 1975*)

Again passing the coal yard, the 10.00 Bradford Exchange/King's Cross (diverted on a Sunday) brings the rare sight of a Class 47, and particularly Mk2 coaches, towards Shipley. (*23 November 1975*)

Somewhat later, but in the same position, the 19.45 Forster Square to King's Cross 'electric' service is dragged all the way to Leeds by a Class 47, then a daily sight! Shipley Goods 'box has gone, and the coal yard has ceased operation. (See also this same train at Forster Square) (*July 1990*)

Pre-electrification local services were in the hands of Pacer units. A Class 144 in Metro livery (and Metrotrain branding) passes the scrap yard. Note the unrestricted growth of lineside vegetation. (*1 August 1992*)

Most unusually, 80080 was used over a protracted period during the winter of 1992/93 to 'train-up' footplate crews in the handling of steam engines, so that there would be no shortage of drivers and firemen for future steam specials. One of these turns is illustrated here; more coaches were picked up in Bradford and the longer train then headed north over the Settle & Carlisle, if I remember correctly. (*20 February 1993*)

Duchess of Hamilton is also heading for Carlisle on the 'Cumbrian Mountain Express', steam having come on in Bradford, though the excursion originated elsewhere. (*18 September 1993*)

The following week saw *Sir Nigel Gresley* appear from the north and run to Bradford with the strangely-named 'The New Inn Farewell' on a glorious evening. (*25 September 1993*)

Post-electrification, the running lines were much more effectively screened from the yard (now named Crossley-Evans) which now had gated entry. Class 333 units now rule the roost. (*6 June 2005*)

In later years Crossley-Evans extended their yard into the ex-coal yard area, and for several years ran train loads of scrap metal down to Cardiff Tidal on a regular basis. An Advenza Rail Class 47 is about to set off with seven loaded wagons, though within five years this traffic ceased to travel by rail. (*5 December 2008*)

With Crossley-Evans' tracks obviously out of use, the 06.30 Forster Square to King's Cross passes the ever-burgeoning growth of lineside trees. (*5 August 2015*)

With Guiseley Junction 'box in the background and the Ilkley line clearly splitting from the four tracks towards Leeds, the Idle branch freight climbs steadily up the valley side. (*30 August 1968*)

This is Idle Goods Shed and yard, with the old station in the distance above the rear cab of the diesel. The branch closed on 7 October 1968, with this shot taken just four months before, on 6 June 1968.

Back at Guiseley Junction on a misty day, a 'Peak' class diesel accelerates the *Thames-Clyde Express* towards Leeds, where it will reverse and head for St Pancras. (*1 March 1975*)

Guiseley Junction again, but looking the other way at a full set of semaphore signals, a four-track main line, double-track on the Ilkley line and a beautiful clear day. The 4-car Morecambe train will reverse into platform 1 at Shipley before proceeding further. (*20 April 1976*)

Guess where! Four tracks have become three, a signal post has gone and the Ilkley line is about to be singled. None of which bothers the double-headed train of chemical tanks (Classes 47+40) heading east. (*20 December 1981*)

By now the line towards Leeds has been only double-track for years, as the early Skipton–London train rushes towards Thackley tunnel with a full set of East Coast Mk4 stock behind a distant Class 91 *Skyfall*. (*6 August 2015*)

Chapter Four

Leeds

NEW LEEDS becomes NEWER LEEDS

The pre-1968 Legacy

The station that had opened on 1 May 1967 had been a compromise compared to the original 1957 rebuilding plan. Work on this had commenced in October 1959, only to be stopped in July 1961 by the curtailment of government expenditure, and a cheaper alternative design was therefore sought. The compromise plan was therefore restarted in March 1963 and completed in May 1967.

From a railway operating point of view, the proposed flyover that would have diverted Central station's traffic towards the new City station was abandoned, as was the provision of two extra tracks at the western approaches. For passengers, the new design incorporated subway connections to the new platforms; a wide and bright subway with new toilet facilities, yes, but still a subway, with step access to the platforms. (By 1968 Leeds City Council had been invited more than once to contribute to the estimated £30,000 cost of replacing these steps with escalators; nothing came of these pleas.) Passengers also enjoyed very little canopy cover over the longer platforms, this being aggravated by some of the through platforms being split so that two trains could stand at the same platform simultaneously, inevitably causing part of longer trains to occupy space beyond the covered section of the train shed. (It did not go unnoticed either that the parcels platforms were covered in their entirety!). These two contentious provisions lasted throughout the lifetime of the 1967 version of the station. The original plan had also included a multi-storey car park over the east end. This too was discarded and a moderate facility created at ground level at the west end by allowing parking within part of the parcels area and inside the un-refurbished North Concourse, access being gained from Aire Street.

During the building period the BR Chairman Dr Beeching published his famous Report, anticipating that the government would accept, more or less totally, that the proposed closure of the many stations and lines around the West Riding that he had identified, would be implemented. Most did of course close, mainly in the years 1965/66/67 and the expected result of these would be to reduce local traffic in the Leeds/Bradford area. (See the list of those stations affected in the Introduction.)

Rather fewer passenger trains might ensure smoother station operations, and in addition as much freight as possible was to be diverted around the station directly to the existing goods yards. Some of the long-distance trains (Liverpool/Newcastle for instance) could be re-routed so that reversal in the station was avoided, and if diesel locos 'ran round' other expresses in order to change direction rather than providing a new engine, light engine movements would not be required either, again simplifying station working.

Hence, despite only four tracks instead of six at the western end, and the lack of a flyover, the remodelled Whitehall Curve – plus the new colour light signalling – was expected to cope with traffic flows for the foreseeable future. (The computerised train describer equipment in the new signal box (that replaced 18 manual 'boxes in the vicinity) was not ready in time for the 1 May opening, installation taking place the following year.) At this time 500 trains passed through Leeds on a typical day, carrying an estimated 2.75 million passengers per year (though the number of parcels dealt with was well in excess of this!).

Not all of Dr Beeching's local proposals came to pass however. For instance, when the Leeds/Bradford/Ilkley line had been put forward for closure, the Ilkley Railway Passenger Association was formed to fight to keep the line open. In this they were successful, and today the line is both busy and electrified!

Post-1968 Developments

The year 1968 proved to be highly significant for the railways. Not only did steam traction on BR lines come to an end, but a Transport Act passed through Parliament that was, in time, to transform the fortunes of many rail services Dr Beeching had had in mind for closure, and others as well, on a national basis. This Act introduced the possibility of Government (or local Council) subsidy for services which, though loss-making at the time, were seen to be socially necessary. These should not only survive, but be promoted and developed with a view to reducing the subsidy provided. The West Riding did, at this time have a number of such services deemed worthy of support and the County Council lost no time in applying for Grants. Those relevant to Leeds services are detailed below.

One-year Grants for 1969		Two-year Grants for 1969, 1970	
Leeds/Harrogate	£223,000	Leeds/Bradford	£169,000
Leeds/Huddersfield	£89,000	Leeds/Goole	£98,000
Leeds/Morecambe	£251,000	Leeds/York	£136,000
Leeds/Barnsley/Sheff'd	£402,000	Leeds/Doncaster	£56,000
Leeds/Rotherham/Sheff'd	£107,000		
Leeds/Liverpool	£211,000		
Leeds/Hull	£309,000		

As an unresolved closure proposal on 1 January 1969, the Leeds/Bradford/Ilkley services were grant-aided for the time being under transitional powers in the 1968 Act. In 1972 the Minister eventually refused to allow these services to be withdrawn, and grant-aid was awarded subject to some re-routing of Bradford/Ilkley trains via Apperley Junction (reverse), but only as far as

Guiseley where the Bradford train terminated and passengers were to change onto a Leeds/Ilkley service to reach Ilkley, an arrangement soon to be superseded.

By and large, the annual grants for the above lines decreased in successive years after 1969, as BR and local Councils made efforts to improve the 'saved' services. Increased patronage, and therefore revenue, led to smaller grants in subsequent years. Of course, if the aided service did not improve during the one- or two-year period, the Minister would issue formal closure notices. This grant system operated for the years 1969–1974 inclusive. However, the Local Government Act of 1974 set up a system of supplementary grants, and these came into effect on 1 April 1975.

Halfway through this period, in July 1972, the Eastern Region launched, in Leeds, a major campaign to secure the long-term future of the entire network of local passenger lines in the West Riding. At the time this network consisted of 452 route miles over 15 routes linking 78 stations, and was underwritten by government grants totalling £2 million per year. The main thrust to this campaign was to create greater public awareness of specific services, and identify the fifteen routes to be promoted, by name.

Principal steps to generate new interest in the local rail services were:

(a) a variety of travel incentives including 'Bullseye Zone Tickets' valid for 7 days unlimited travel in 6 zones
(b) a large scale advertising campaign in 9 daily and 11 weekly newspapers; also on TV
(c) wide distribution of over 100,000 brochures, including at venues such as shopping areas, department stores etc.
(d) new composite timetables covering all 15 services with a diagrammatic map of the named routes
(e) all literature to include the familiar 'White Rose' county symbol.

(Note; The current Metro map (at the end of this chapter) lists 12 routes (of the original 15) in a similar display, and has its genesis in this West Riding version. Nowadays coverage is confined to West Yorkshire lines and stations, whereas the West Riding version contained what is now South Yorkshire plus bits of North Yorkshire also. The three 'missing' routes covered SY services.)

This campaign was an immediate success. In the first 8 weeks traffic rose by 2.2 per cent – and receipts by 8.9 per cent, and in the 6 months to October 1973 the number of journeys on the 15 routes increased by 150,000 to 2.8 million and revenue by 18 per cent!

From this point onwards, for local rail services there has been no looking back.

West Yorkshire Passenger Transport Executive and the Metro

On 1 April 1974 the West Yorkshire Metropolitan County Council came into being and the old West Riding ceased to exist. West Yorkshire Passenger Transport Executive (WYPTE) was set up at the same time to control and promote railway services under the title Metro, in the region bounded by the five Metropolitan Authorities within West Yorkshire: Leeds, Bradford, Wakefield, Kirklees (Huddersfield) and Calderdale (Halifax). By July 1974 the West Yorkshire County Council had made submissions for grant-aided services in 1975/76, though it was not possible for the WYPTE to take over responsibility for these services on 1 January 1975 as originally intended, and Government agreed that this should be deferred until 1 January 1976. Henceforward, the WYPTE took over from where the Eastern Region left off – with a vengeance.

The Government's Transport Supplementary Grant (TSG) awarded to West Yorkshire for 1975/76 was £14.7 million (with the new South Yorkshire administration receiving £6.5 million). These totals included bus subsidies, road maintenance and capital projects as well as rail subsidies, and were well below the sums submitted by the Metropolitan Counties!

As from 1 January 1976 WYPTE began to support the entire rail passenger network, though the deficit on services from Leeds to Ilkley, Keighley, Knottingley and Todmorden was to be met temporarily whilst their future role was assessed, as the overall rail deficit for West Yorkshire amounted to £3.7 million in the financial year 1975/76. Another initial difficulty was that some of the old West Riding routes crossed over into both North, and South Yorkshire, and 'their' contribution to through services from Leeds took some time to resolve.

Subsequent TSGs for West Yorkshire for the next two years were as follows;

| 1976/77 | £12.4 million |
| 1977/78 | £11.6 million |

and as the downward trend seemed likely to continue, WYPTE looked urgently at ways to increase revenue even if this meant, in the short-to-medium term, extra expenditure on new infrastructure and refurbished rolling stock.

Bradford City Council had sponsored the re-opening of Baildon station (on the Forster Square/Ilkley line) as early as January 1973, and Leeds' first thoughts in this direction were to open new stations at Hemsworth and Fitzwilliam (on the Wakefield to Doncaster Line) to serve large housing developments, though this would not be a quick move. Also under consideration was the extension of the 'MetroCard', available on WYPTE's road services, to cover trains as well, though this also proved to be difficult. However, as the Leeds/Bradford area had been the pioneer district when d.m.u.s were first introduced in 1954, thoughts also turned to the refurbishment of its fleet of 286 long-in-the-tooth first

generation d.m.u.s. (This was a cheaper option than buying equivalent new vehicles, which in any case did not exist!). Hence, at the WYPTE's initiative the entire output of Doncaster Works' programme of refurbished units (94 per year) was promised to West Yorkshire; over a period of three years this would therefore convert all the fleet. The prototype 'Demonstrator' units were available from July 1974 and visited towns on the Eastern Region. The striking livery was white, with a waist-level band in blue, on which was carried the WYPTE symbol. These new vehicles (at least they looked new!) promoted both the Metro and rail travel, and were a relatively quick way to encourage extra passengers. Gaining planning approval for new stations (and finding the money) was slower, and it was to be 1982 before Fitzwilliam, Deighton, Crossflatts and Slaithwaite were opened, followed by Bramley in 1983, and it was 1984 before Saltaire began contributing revenue from the new station. (Hemsworth never did make it! Saltaire was declared a World Heritage Site in 2001.) The process had however begun, and by 2005 the grand total of twenty-three stations had been added to the Metro network, with further possibilities in the pipeline.

However successful the rolling stock refurbishment programme was, it was still in essence only a stop-gap measure to extend the life of old vehicles for a few more years before alternative stock came on the scene. BR's first offering here was a 3-car diesel-electric unit (Class 210) of high specification – and hence too costly – to be of interest to WYPTE (or indeed others amongst the six English Metropolitan Councils).

Private industry was offering various types of railbus, but these 4-wheeled vehicles did not have the carrying capacity to interest the PTEs either. BR's next, cheaper, alternative was a 2-car 4-wheeled lightweight railbus (Class 140), the prototype of which had a press run from Leeds to Ilkley and back in the late spring of 1981 before trials in public service in June on the Leeds/Marsden route. By the end of the following year (1982) d.m.u. maintenance costs were swallowing over 30 per cent of West Yorkshire's rail subsidy and their replacement with a cheaper-to-run alternative was becoming urgent. WYPTE therefore signed a letter of intent to purchase all twenty units similar to the Class 140 prototype that had undergone trials there. The units on offer, Class 141, were however to a BR specification which did not meet WYPTE's requirements too closely (having not been consulted over them!). It was therefore with some reluctance that the PTE accepted BR's offer of a two-year trial rental agreement for these units (in which the PTE would only pay for 9½ of the 20) that would give some comparison time if other new units became available. The first unit of these 'Pacers' was delivered on 19 March 1984 and was followed by a demonstration return run between Leeds and Doncaster. All twenty 2-car units were due to be operational from Neville Hill depot in time for the new timetable in May 1985, and were turned out in the PTE livery of Verona green and buttermilk (nineteen arrived; one was retained at Derby for testing).

These 'Pacers', although much cheaper to operate, were narrow-bodied and only provided ninety-four seats (twenty fewer than a first generation 2-car unit) and did nothing to alleviate the overcrowding on commuter services in & out of Leeds. It was no surprise therefore that the PTE committed to better alternatives in 1986, when the first of the Class 144 'Pacer' 2-car railbuses (capacity 122 seats) left Derby Works on 9 August bound for Neville Hill, in the new PTE livery of red and buttermilk. After driver training, these commenced public service between Leeds and

Doncaster on 15 December 1986. Capacity was further increased when 3-car units of Class 144 became available to swell the fleet in 1986/87.

Back in July 1983 the PTE had introduced 'Saver Strips' (twelve journeys for the price of ten) on bus services, and extended these to cover rail usage as well during 1985. A further development in 1985 happened when the MetroCard system finally became valid for both road and rail transport, as from 13 January. In the same year, of the 661 weekday passenger trains now operating within the West Yorkshire, 77 per cent were subsidised by the PTE. In the eight years that the PTE had been supporting local services, patronage (in thousands) had been as below – the later years being recession-hit, particularly 1982/83 which also had severe industrial relations problems;

1976/77	5,670	1977/78	5,583
1979/80	6,470	1980/81	7,458
1981/82	7,537	1982/83	6,093
1983/84	6,564	1984/85	7,040

In 1985/86 it was the case that fares covered 70 per cent of the costs of running the buses, but just 30 per cent of the costs of running the trains. Though *running* costs were comparable for both modes, the disparity is accounted for by the infrastructure costs the PTE had to pay BR. However, with bus deregulation on the horizon during 1986, the 70 per cent figure looked likely to decrease as private bus operators sought to cherry-pick the profitable routes and, in being allowed to do so, effectively dismantle the carefully built-up integration of road and rail services the PTE had been at pains to establish! With Government subsidies becoming ever tighter during recession years, economies looked inevitable on both road and rail. Support had already been withdrawn from the Clayton West branch (on the Penistone line), allowing this to close in January 1983, and the PTE had now to decline support for the Huddersfield/Denby Dale section of the same line; as of 1983 the Penistone line required £6.20 in subsidy for every £1 taken in revenue.

In addition to bus deregulation in October, the abolition of the Metropolitan County Councils was scheduled for April, so that 1986 was an eventful year! However, a new Passenger Transport Authority now oversaw the PTE and in April, immediately backed the policy of replacing rolling stock as quickly as possible. Production designs of the 142 and 143 Class successors to the 141s would be demonstrated in West Yorkshire as soon as they were available, and the Class 150 'Sprinter' d.m.u. would be quickly introduced on the Calder Valley line (York/Bradford/ Manchester). As a further sign of changing times, the 8,000th mast of the East Coast Main Line electrification scheme was 'planted' at the end of platform 7 of Leeds station on 5 August (1986) marking the 'quarter-way stage' of the 400 mile project, and reminding all that the first electric train was due to run to Leeds in October 1989. (BR actually ran a year ahead of schedule; the first test train came in on 11 August 1988, exactly twenty years after BR ran its last steam train!).

Post 'Metropolitan Council' Developments
The PTE, now operating under the wing of the PTA from April 1986, signalled no change in overall policy, though the events of 5 August (mentioned above) caused long-term thinking to come into sharper focus as regards rolling stock for the Leeds–Doncaster local services post-electrification. More immediately, the newly rebuilt Leeds station ticket hall was opened on 15 February 1987, and later in that year three

new stations were added to the network; East Garforth (May), Frizinghall (September), Sandal & Agbrigg (November) on the York & Selby, Airedale and Wakefield lines respectively. On the other hand, possible closure of the Leeds/ Woodlesford/Castleford/Normanton line was avoided by diverting Leeds/ Barnsley/Sheffield trains via Castleford, though Altofts station would still close. At 10.6 million passengers per year the patronage of the various Metro lines was now at its highest since the (much larger) pre-Beeching network, and extra capacity, especially during the daily peaks, was urgently required. To meet this demand, 20 x Class 144, extra Pacers of Class 142 and 6 x Class 150 Sprinter units were on order. Further, ten of these 2-car Class 144 Pacers would be upgraded by the addition of a third (powered) centre car, making a 3-car set with 195 seats. By the May 1988 timetable, improved frequencies on the busiest routes would be introduced to make best use of the new stock, the Airedale & Wharfedale lines being the prime example, where passenger numbers had increased by 58 per cent in just three years!

Another positive move was the retention of the only rural rail service in West Yorkshire, the Huddersfield/Denby Dale/Sheffield route. This was made secure by two economies; the singling of the line and the use of Pacer units, plus BR's new accounting system for such lines; as a further vote of confidence in the line, a new station at Berry Brow was subsequently opened in October 1989.

In the aftermath of bus de-regulation in October 1986, the new PTA had predicted that rail journeys would fall by 10 per cent. However, such was the uncertainty created by the new bus routes and schedules that car usage increased markedly, traffic jams ensued (especially in Leeds) so that commuters turned to rail, *increasing* journeys by 10 per cent! When the Metropolitan County Council ceased to exist, its road building programme died with it, which may also have been a factor in soaring railway patronage, then anticipated to reach 14 million journeys per year if trends continued upwards. To assist in making this prediction valid, further new stations were opened in 1988 at Cononley (North Yorkshire, but on the Airedale line) and Cottingley (Huddersfield line) – both in April, Outwood (July, Wakefield line, where electrification wiring was already in place) and Burley Park (November, Harrogate line), and 1990 saw the reopening of Steeton & Silsden (May, Airedale line) and Walsden (September, Calder Valley line), making no less than sixteen new stations on Metro lines since the formation of the Metro network in 1974 – quite a record.

Unfortunately, once the fleet of Classes 142/144 Pacers had been in service several months, these units began to develop gearbox problems at an alarming rate. They were all covered by a two-year warranty, but their withdrawal for modification put enormous pressure on operating staff, particularly at Neville Hill depot, to keep others running (including 1950s d.m.u.s) so that the timetable could operate. Inevitably this was not always successful and complaints about inappropriate stock, shortened trains, cancelled services, late running, gross overcrowding etc. soon forced the PTA to threaten BR with legal action if a solution was not found with greater urgency. Withholding part of the PTE's payment to BR was discussed, as BR was seen to be 'dragging its feet' over the issue, as they foresaw the modifications not being completed before April 1989.

During this fraught time, WYPTE took delivery on 12 September 1988 of the first of seven Class 155 Super Sprinters, bought directly from the manufacturers (Leyland). The unit was unveiled

officially with a run from Leeds to York, filmed by local TV channels. Intended for Calder Valley services, these were joined by three Class 156 Super Sprinters provided by BR from October, thus enabling the existing Class 150 Sprinters to operate on the Leeds/ Barnsley/Sheffield route.

Again regrettably, all the seven new '155's were temporarily withdrawn by BR for safety checks in December. A fault had been discovered in the automatic door mechanism on Western Region units and checks were deemed necessary on all such vehicles, which were returned to West Yorkshire by 15 May 1989.

Just to add insult to injury WYPTE had, by the end of 1989, also ordered ten 2-car Class 158 Express units for delivery in early 1991, but production was already forty weeks behind schedule! (This was largely due to the confusion arising out of the sale of BREL's Derby Works, where the units were being built.)

A further complication to running a timetable with different classes of d.m.u.s was that drivers had to be 'passed out' on each of the types he was expected to drive. Hence, if the depot was forced to make a last-minute change of rolling stock (a not infrequent occurrence at the time) but the driver (who would be waiting on the platform for the empty stock to arrive) was not 'qualified' to drive it, then either the train was cancelled or substantially delayed whilst an appropriate driver could be found! Nightmare.

Meanwhile the simmering row between West Yorkshire and BR about Pacer gearboxes, the withdrawal of the '155' Super Sprinters and the late delivery of the order for Class 158s, all led to the PTA withholding three Section 20 payments to BR totalling nearly £188,000 effectively 'fining' BR for supplying units that were not doing what they were supposed to be doing!

Whilst all this was happening, the programme of station improvements continued. During 1987 for instance, Halifax received £30,000-worth of attention; Keighley had its waiting room renovated and a stone shelter erected on the platform, Normanton was given an environmental face-lift, Micklefield gained easier ramp access to the York platform and Shipley had a computer-controlled train information system installed. Infrastructure was being updated as well; in 1988 the ex-LNWR viaduct line into Leeds was closed and Geldard Road Junction remodelled, as was (to some extent) Whitehall Junction – both with a view to the forthcoming electrification of the line from Doncaster and London. In this connection, overhead wiring was installed right into Leeds station, though only platforms 5, 6, 8 and the east-end bay platform 4 were so provided along with their respective approach lines.

Leeds' big day – 'E-Day' – arrived on Thursday, 11 August 1988 when a test train came in behind electric loco 91 004, and some regular London passenger services began to be hauled electrically from the following day by the Class 89 prototype. The service was upgraded again the following year (1989) when new coaching stock came into use and the Class 91s took full control. Local trains to Doncaster continued to be operated by d.m.u.s however until 3 July 1990 when, at long last, 4-car e.m.u.s of Class 307 began to replace Pacers for welcome use elsewhere. Unlike the new London expresses, these e.m.u.s were decidedly old, being cast-offs from Network South East and dating from the mid-1950s! On 9 July the PTA ordered three new Class 321 units from BREL to replace the six ancient '307's, though delivery would not be until 1991.

Still in 1990, the PTA gained Government credit approval for its North Leeds electrification scheme, which involved the Airedale line as far as Skipton and the Wharfedale line to Ilkley, both from Leeds and from Bradford. The plan had been to reach Shipley and Bradford from Leeds by 1993, to reach Ilkley and Skipton in 1994, and of course re-signal the entire area, then controlled manually with semaphore signals. Unfortunately this Government credit agreement only extended to infrastructure work and did not cover the estimated 14 x 3-car units necessary to work the services, leaving the PTA with a question mark as to how to fund these. More than a year later no satisfactory way had been found of buying the PTE's share of thirteen of the fourteen new electric trains needed, and only in December 1991 did the Department of Transport agree to the PTE's proposal to lease the trains, having turned down a similar proposal twelve months earlier. By this time the issue of rail privatisation was coming to the boil and the leasing company wanted guarantees from the PTE that it was unable to give, since it was at least possible that the PTE itself might be abolished on privatisation! This impasse continued until mid-1992, when BR eventually promised that second-hand Class 308 e.m.u.s would be made available if no leasing finance could be agreed, effectively 'saving' the entire project, as the infrastructure contracts (suspended since 1990) could now be let. The promise of twenty-one 30-year-old Class 308s, redundant from the Fenchurch Street/ Shoeburyness line was however seen as a safety net simply to ensure electric trains would run beneath electric wires, though these units would need replacement within a short time. Dé jàvu. Doncaster electrics all over again.

WYPTE therefore broke off negotiations with Hunslet for some of its new trains, to give itself some time for reflection until the legislative position became clearer. At this point it may be instructive to list the rolling stock allocation at the disposal of Neville Hill depot with which to operate all the local services as of May 1992.

19 x 2-car Class 141 Pacers	7 x 2-car Class 155 Sprinters
28 x 2-car Class 142 Pacers	25 x 2-car Class 156 Super Sprinters
13 x 2-car Class 144 Pacers	32 x 2-car Class 158 Express
10 x 3-car Class 144 Pacers	3 x 4-car Class 321 e.m.u.s

290 vehicles in all.

Although the North Leeds project had now been substantially delayed, the infrastructure work now got under way; track alterations were made at Skipton and a new washing plant installed at the stabling point long used by Pacers; Shipley gained the long-awaited extra platform and footbridge connection, Bradford Forster Square rebuilding was completed, and the layout at Guiseley significantly altered, whilst at Leeds station platforms 1, 2, 3, 11, and 12 and a freight line were electrified, to name but a few of the works. In all, thirteen signal boxes were closed with the routes now controlled from three panels on the Leeds power 'box. With the project well behind schedule, the Ilkley route was the first to be energised on 23 January 1995, with the final stretch between Saltaire and Skipton in the spring. Services were partially electrified from the 17 May timetable change with a fully electric service from 25 September (together with increased frequencies), after sufficient training of drivers and conductors had taken place. The Class 308 units themselves had all been through Doncaster Works, overhauled, reduced from 4-car to 3-car sets and turned out in Metro livery of red and buttermilk, but now branded Regional Railways.

In parallel with the introduction of electric local trains outlined above, privatisation of the railways had begun, though was not yet complete nationally. However, WYPTE reported in April 1994 that the cost of its rail services had practically *tripled* for the year 1994/95, Railtrack's track access charges being the main culprit, and these had hit the infrastructure work on the North Leeds scheme particularly hard. Extra Government Grants would cover the first year, but after that…? The original pre-privatisation 'promise' that Bradford would get six electric trains to London was cast aside, and finally resulted in East Coast Trains supplying just one through service, the entire train (including electric loco with pantograph lowered) being diesel hauled from Leeds to Forster Square! (The electricity supply on the Airedale route was insufficient to power a full-length express; Skipton's single through service to Kings' Cross was provided by an HST diesel unit all the way to London!).

Perhaps to some peoples' surprise, Leeds won the 1996 'Station of the Year' awarded by Rotary International, the presentation being made by British Rail Chairman John Welsby on 8 March. Hanging baskets bedecking the platforms helped of course as did the station garden (located against the buffer stops of platforms 2/3 and opened by Sir Jimmy Savile in March 1994), plus the new lounge gracing platform 12 – the busy TransPennine platform. Only four Train Operating Companies provided all the passenger services; Regional Railways North East (70 per cent majority), East Coast (20 per cent) with Cross Country and Midland Main Line 5 per cent each. When built in 1967, the station handled twenty-four westbound trains in the evening rush hour, in 1996 this had grown to twenty-eight (with reduced capacity since the viaduct line had been closed), and west-end congestion was now becoming critical.

During 1997, however, WYPTE began to have cause for deep dissatisfaction with the standard of service provided by RRNE, with driver shortages being the main factor in increasing levels of complaint throughout the year. A highlight, on the other hand, was the naming (in foul weather!) on 25 June of Virgin power car 43 153 as *The English Riviera* before taking out *The Devonian*, the 08.15 Leeds/Paignton.

On 20 November 1997 came the biggest news of the year, with the announcement by the Chief Executive of Railtrack, Gerald Corbett, of the 'Leeds 2000' (or 'Leeds 1st' as it became known) redevelopment plan for Leeds station. Costed at £165 million, the plan was formally approved by the Railtrack Board on 15 January 1999, with completion planned for the end of 2001. This envisaged the total rebuild of a station that had already undergone recent significant alterations; firstly for the electrification of the East Coast main line to Leeds, followed by further electrification of the suburban lines to Skipton and Ilkley. Despite the fact that it was obviously in need of greater capacity, the totality of the rebuilding was a most welcome decision. By the beginning of 2002 the scheme was scheduled to deliver the following major improvements:

- widening of the west-end approaches to accommodate six tracks, all bi-directionally signalled, making 40 paths an hour available instead of 28, together with increased speed from 15 to 25mph
- double-tracking of the freight line around the Whitehall Junction – Engine Shed Junction section, hence also doubling freight capacity north-south

- provision of 17 platforms, all electrically wired, 5 more than previously
- virtually all track, pointwork, ballast and signalling to be new, with signal control being transferred to York
- new higher roof to be installed, giving brighter and more spacious train shed than before
- more platform length to be under canopy
- west-end footbridge to be escalator-connected to all platforms, plus stairs and lifts, making all platforms accessible to those with disabilities. An extra footbridge at east end (stairs only) to be provided also. (No subway!)
- North Concourse to be completely refurbished; to contain retail outlets and cafés. To be accessible again from City Square, and via a new main entrance created at the north-west corner. This entrance to have road access and face an adjacent new multi-storey car park.

It was remarked upon in the Introduction that any rebuild of Leeds station would be subject to considerable physical restraints, and it is appropriate here to enumerate these.

When the NER and the LNWR extended the line westwards from Marsh Lane (the original 1834 terminus of the Leeds & Selby Railway one mile east of the central area) this new line was built entirely on a brick-arched viaduct to a site alongside, but south of, the Midland Railway's Wellington terminal station, to a new through station called Leeds (New) – which was opened in 1879. both stations were orientated east/west; Leeds (New) being confined on its south side by the Leeds & Liverpool Canal basin and elevated above it by the viaduct. To the immediate north of the adjacent Wellington station (not on the viaduct and therefore a few feet below it) the river Aire approached central Leeds from the west, before being turned south and flowing through the brick arches (under both stations) to emerge at the eastern end of the canal basin, which connected into the Aire via single lock. In addition, two busy throughfares, Neville Street and Swinegate, passed north/south beneath the arches at the eastern end of the New station.

It was therefore this site that had been rebuilt previously in 1967, and from the above description it is apparent that Railtrack's second total rebuild of Leeds station would have to be completed on exactly the same footprint as the existing railway.

To assist the completion of work within the station area overnight, a temporary single platform station was constructed – Leeds (Whitehall) – on the freight only Whitehall Junction/Engine Shed Junction curve, operational from 26 September 1999 onwards between midnight and 05.00. Initially used by Manchester Airport trains, later by trains from the Normanton direction, this enabled night-time possession of Leeds station. Free shuttle buses connected these trains with Leeds station. Use of this facility ceased on 25 February 2002, and the platform was later demolished.

Unfortunately, for various reasons, 'Leeds 1st' overran considerably, most notably when a 7-day possession over the Christmas period in 2000 turned into a 22-day nightmare. The cost escalated substantially also, with the original £165 million leaping to £245 million by the time of the official completion on 1 August 2002 (Yorkshire Day!).

Meanwhile, although the North Leeds electrified lines immediately improved patronage, the Class 308 units were merely a stop-gap provision, and in early 1998 RRNE selected Siemens to build new units to replace them. The order was for 16 x 3-car sets based on the 'Heathrow Express' Class 332 units, and would be known as Class 333. They were to be built in Spain

with German traction motors; first deliveries were scheduled for mid-2000, and would be maintained at a modernised Neville Hill depot.

Forward therefore to 10 March 2000 when the first of these new sets arrived from Siemens. Unlike the Class 321s, which simply came 'up the road' from Doncaster, the Class 333s came through the Channel Tunnel by rail, pulled by electric locos. The initial unit was then hauled from Dollands Moor to Wembley, from whence it was worked forward to Wakefield Europort next day for onward travel to Neville Hill. The others followed suit in due course. As delivered, the '333's had a seating capacity of 260 per 3-car unit, but WYPTE quickly secured funding for eight further intermediate trailers to enable half the fleet to be strengthened to 4-car sets, seating 340. Being very similar to the '332's, some staff training had already taken place at Old Oak Common 'Heathrow Express' depot, before overnight testing on the Leeds/ Ilkley/ Skipton and Leeds/Doncaster routes commenced in April. Interestingly, units 333003/005 were tested during the night of July 9/10 in the Skipton area as a 6-car set, something that as far as the author is aware, has never since been repeated! (Nor as 2 x 4-car sets either). Later in the year day-time testing had begun and by the end of 2001 all sixteen units had been delivered.

The first 'in service' passenger run came on 23 January 2001 when 333010 powered the official launch train, the 10.42 Leeds/Bradford Forster Square. By February 26 all sixteen sets were commissioned and the life-expired '308' units began to be withdrawn, four of their number being sent to Shoeburyness for storage on 18 January. The 'Leeds 1st' project had overrun into January 2001 blocking access to Neville Hill, and several instances were recorded of '308's and '333's 'stranded' at Skipton or Bradford having to be diesel-hauled to Neville Hill via Gascoigne

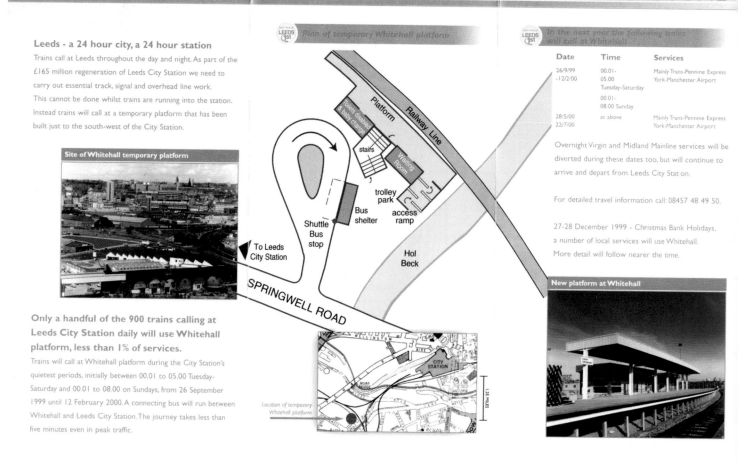

Leeds - a 24 hour city, a 24 hour station

Trains call at Leeds throughout the day and night. As part of the £165 million regeneration of Leeds City Station we need to carry out essential track, signal and overhead line work. This cannot be done whilst trains are running into the station. Instead trains will call at a temporary platform that has been built just to the south-west of the City Station.

Site of Whitehall temporary platform

Only a handful of the 900 trains calling at Leeds City Station daily will use Whitehall platform, less than 1% of services.

Trains will call at Whitehall platform during the City Station's quietest periods, initially between 00.01 to 05.00 Tuesday-Saturday and 00.01 to 08.00 on Sundays, from 26 September 1999 until 12 February 2000. A connecting bus will run between Whitehall and Leeds City Station. The journey takes less than five minutes even in peak traffic.

LEEDS 1st Plan of temporary Whitehall platform

Location of temporary Whitehall platform

LEEDS 1st In the next year the following trains will call at Whitehall

Date	Time	Services
26/9/99 -12/2/00	00.01-05.00 Tuesday-Saturday 00.01-08.00 Sunday	Mainly Trans-Pennine Express York-Manchester Airport
28/5/00 22/7/00	as above	Mainly Trans-Pennine Express York-Manchester Airport

Overnight Virgin and Midland Mainline services will be diverted during these dates too, but will continue to arrive and depart from Leeds City Station.

For detailed travel information call: 08457 48 49 50.

27-28 December 1999 - Christmas Bank Holidays, a number of local services will use Whitehall. More detail will follow nearer the time.

New platform at Whitehall

(Railtrack publication)

Wood. On 21 December (2000) all three Class 321/9s were serviced at Skipton, again due to the engineering work at Leeds. In March 2001 unit 333004 was a surprise visitor to Doncaster, and the '308' fleet was down to eight units. The remaining handful were withdrawn on 23 August, though 308157/158 were kept in operational condition to run a railtour in October.

In preparation for the '333's being strengthened to four cars, the Ilkley line was closed May 26-28 2001 whilst platform lengthening work was carried out. By mid-December the first of the extra vehicles had arrived, and 333001 became the first 4-car set in public use, working the 11.30 Leeds/Bradford on 2 March 2002; at about the same time, an order was placed for a further eight

'4th' cars, for delivery in late 2003, thus eventually equipping the entire fleet. By the beginning of the summer timetable 2002, 333001-008 were all 4-car sets.

Whilst Leeds station was still in turmoil (though it should not have been by now), Great North Eastern Railways supplied a landmark event on 8 April 2002. This was the arrival into Leeds from Doncaster of the first test run of a 14-coach + 2 x power cars Regional Eurostar set in readiness for the introduction, in the summer timetable, of a regular service to London with these units. Consequently the initial revenue-earning service (the 07.05 from King's Cross) arrived into Leeds on 5 June, after a special demonstration run southbound seven days earlier.

In the timetable no less than eleven services on the Leeds route were formed of Eurostar stock with GNER drivers, whereas these trains had been driven elsewhere by Eurostar UK's own staff. It was now possible to reach London in one minute under two hours! The extreme length of these sets restricted their access to platforms 8 or 11 at Leeds (and to 1 or 6 at King's Cross).

The original concept of services through the Channel Tunnel had included through workings to the north of England, though these never materialised. (Neither did the 'Nightstar' sleeping car services, despite coaching stock for these being built at huge expense, never to turn a wheel. These were subsequently stored (largely on secure MOD property at Kineton) only to be sold in their entirety to Canada at a knock-down price of $130 million!). The seven Regional Eurostars (for the proposed north of England workings) had themselves been stored out-of-use at North Pole depot in west London for five years before GNER began using three sets from this pool to operate services to York as from 28 May 2000 and until 1 June 2002, when the units were switched to the Leeds run. However, with GNER's leasing arrangement with Eurostar UK expiring at the end of 2005, these prestige sets ceased to grace Leeds' new station when the timetable changed on 10 December. Thereafter, GNER continued to improve its Leeds service, introducing a half-hourly frequency from 21 May 2007, giving no less than sixty-five trains per weekday between Leeds and London compared with only thirty-seven when it began its franchise in 1996!

More recently, in July 2014, the station was invaded by an unexpectedly large contingent of cycling enthusiasts! On Saturday, 5 July the Tour de France's *Grand Depart* was from Leeds, Stage 1 finishing in Harrogate, and an estimated 60,000 extra passengers descended on the station in the hope of reaching Harrogate. The regular services were augmented by the hiring-in of two extra loco-hauled trains performing 'shuttle runs' to and from Harrogate, but long queues nevertheless formed. Stage 2 the following day was from York to Sheffield via the Calder Valley and the two extra train sets were employed taking spectators to Hebden Bridge, where all the major roads in the area were closed.

Slightly earlier, on 1 April 2014 and having existed for forty years, the WYPTE was formally abolished. The new body responsible for transport policy in the region is now named the West Yorkshire Combined Authority, though the 'Metro' branding remains unaltered.

As of 2015, there seems to be no immediate prospect of any further lines being electrified. Plans have been made, and subsequently un-made, to energise the busy TransPennine route (the prime candidate), but all the other commuter lines from Leeds look destined to be worked by Pacer or Sprinter units for some time yet, though these are already nearly 30 years old. In this context, significantly, Pacer unit 144 012 has been given a substantial up-grade to its interior by Porterbrook (the Rolling Stock Company). Thus modified to comply with forthcoming mobility regulations (and including a wheelchair-friendly toilet), this demonstrator – christened 'Evolution Pacer' – ran trials from Neville Hill during August 2015 over the Leeds/Castleford/ Knottingley/ Pontefract/Wakefield route. It remains to be seen whether this will be duplicated and prolong the lives of these aging vehicles. Five Class 322 e.m.u.s have been cascaded from ScotRail to supplement the three Class 321 units (both Classes now 25 years old) and the newer '333' units on the three routes that are electrified, and the sole Skipton/ King's Cross through service (now worked by Virgin Trains East Coast) is at last headed by a Class 91 loco (Mon-Fri; it's still an HST at weekends). Current train operating companies besides Virgin, and therefore responsible for all passenger workings in & out of Leeds, are Northern, TransPennine Express (both franchises expiring at the end of March 2016), Cross Country and East Midlands Trains.

Although Leeds' station was completely rebuilt structurally, that has not stopped further developments taking place, or being planned, since then. A new ticket office was opened on 22 January 2004 between the North and South Concourses, replacing the earlier facility, and in 2008 the manned ticket barriers were replaced by automatic gates. A project that was completed in early 2016 is, of course, the new south entrance to Leeds station, built scenically right on top of the River Aire and connecting directly onto the west-end overbridge that accesses all platforms. This is a welcome addition; previous entrances either faced north, or more recently west. A warm, sunny ambience at a station entrance is always more enticing than one in the shade!

Leeds is the second busiest station outside the London area, after Birmingham New Street, and with 17 platforms is the largest (by number of platforms) outside London.

Of these, 11 are terminal (or bay) platforms and 6 are through platforms, though as most are also sub-divided e.g. 1a, 1b, 1c and so on, there are actually 47 platform designations. To cope with ever-increasing passenger numbers, plans are being drawn up to add extra platforms alongside platform 1 on part of the car parking area (on the site of the original Wellington station). Leeds is also a named terminus for the 'HS2' project, though exactly where and when this station – Leeds New Lane – will be located, is a matter of conjecture. However, given the lengthy time-scale proposed for this project (New Lane to open in 2032!) it is hardly surprising that moves are already afoot to propose alternatives. The West & North Yorkshire Chamber of Commerce has, for instance, put forward a scheme for an integrated single station serving both HS2 plus all current railways within an expanded version of the present station. This would, basically, add a 2-track HS2 station onto the south side of the 2002 station, approached on a new elevated viaduct from the west and depart eastwards, also on a new elevated viaduct towards Marsh Lane, parallel to the current eastern exit.

Doubtless this will not be the last word on the subject!

Looking backwards for a change, two surviving buildings from Leeds' early railway history have recently been recognised by the Leeds Civic Trust with the award of Blue Plaques. The first was fixed on 25 July 2011 to the only remaining wagon hoist that operated in what was Wellington Street Goods Depot, and which started work in the 1850s. In 2012 a further plaque was unveiled on 20 November; this time on an engine roundhouse of the Leeds & Thirsk Railway dating from roughly 1848, jointly with a similar semi-roundhouse of a slightly later date, both located on their original site in Wellington Road, and both still in commercial use.

Leeds' railway history stretches back much further however. The Middleton Railway was authorised by Act of Parliament (as a waggon-way) in 1758, to carry coals from Middleton Colliery into central Leeds. A brief resumé of its early history is as follows:- horse drawn until 1812; steam to 1835, horse again to 1866 then steam thereafter, converted from 4 ft 1 in gauge to standard 4 ft 8½ in in 1881, connected to Midland Railway main line by the Balm Road branch in 1894. When freight traffic finally became negligible in the late 1950s, a Preservation

Society was formed from University staff and students, who operated a passenger service on 20 June 1960 – for one week only! – before efforts were redirected to running commercial freight trains over the Balm Road branch and onto British Railways, from 1 September 1960. This traffic decreased gradually during the 1960s, so that a regular passenger service commenced on 30 June 1969 between Hunslet Moor and Middleton Park, which shortly afterwards (1971) passed under the new M621 motorway via an 80m tunnel. Headquarters were moved to Moor Road in 1983, which year also saw the end of all freight operations. Moor Road terminus has grown considerably since then, culminating in the opening of the Engine House in 2007. In 2008 an Early Day Motion was tabled in Parliament to mark the 250th anniversary of the passing of the 1758 Act, and congratulating the Middleton Railway on its continuous operation of the line ever since. In 2010 the Society celebrated fifty years of running services over the line.

The railway currently operates from Moor Road station to Park Halt, just under a mile further south; an extension into Middleton Park is proposed but is a long-term objective. Just to the south of the motorway tunnel, the Dartmouth branch joins the main route; this short stub once connected various local metal industries with the main route. It is still in operation for special events, and has in recent years also been used for training main line track workers.

The former *Thames-Clyde Express* (no longer titled) heads west and passes the new road system still in a state of flux. The roundhouse in the background (above the engine) was built by the Leeds & Thirsk Railway in the 1840s. It now sports a Civic Trust blue plaque. (*25 March 1978*)

A little later *Green Arrow* is on the same track with a Settle & Carlisle special. The power station on the horizon did not last much longer. (*25 March 1978*)

Same location, but here two 2-car Class 142 Pacers approach in Regional Railways livery. (*25 September 1990*)

Also coming into Leeds from the Aire Valley lines, the Class 308 unit forms an interesting contrast with the previous scene. (*5 April 1997*)

Moving slightly nearer in towards Leeds, a Class 144 Pacer passes the site of Holbeck Low Level station. The abutment that carried the High Level line and station is also in view. (*18 April 1987*)

Closer still, at Whitehall Junction *Kolhapur* heads for Carlisle with an excursion from York. (*21 March 1987*)

Whitehall Junction again, but now the Doncaster line (but not yet the Aire Valley line) has been electrified as a Class 47 runs solo towards Copley Hill. Most large buildings seen here are now demolished. (*22 June 1989*)

A Class 142 Pacer leaves Leeds on the four-track (later six-track) curve at Whitehall triangle. Recently transferred from Cornwall, these units were known as 'Skippers' in the South-West. (*23 October 1989*)

The temporary station Leeds (Whitehall) was built more or less exactly where the previous shot was taken from. See also the information leaflet's diagram. *29 July 2000 (J.W. Holroyd)*)

A view along the single, temporary platform. *29 July 2000. (J.W. Holroyd)*

Train 1E79, a Liverpool/Newcastle express, is 'Peak'-hauled into Leeds. Note the parcels stock in the ex-Wellington section. (*2 August 1974*)

On a damp day, a Class 47 is about to depart on train 1A16, the *Yorkshire Pullman*, for King's Cross. The Dragonara Hotel dominates the skyline. (*30 July 1974*)

A special railtour from/to Manchester via Sheffield & Leeds is featured here; Midland compound 1000 ahead of *Green Arrow*. (*3 May 1980*)

Union of South Africa is temporarily parked on the goods lines whilst transferring itself and two coaches to York. (See also Keighley, Airedale Line section). (*14 September 1985*)

In the early days of East Coast electrification into Leeds, a special from King's Cross runs in behind a Class 86/2 loco – a rare type to visit Leeds. Parcels vans occupying the old 'Wellington' section were still a common sight at this time. (*18 February 1989*)

Emerging from the confines of the train shed, the unique 89 001 recently named *Avocet* by Prime Minister Margaret Thatcher, heads the 16.00 through to King's Cross. The name only lasted until June 1992. (*23 March 1989*)

A 'modified' HST (i.e. equipped with a pair of buffers) leaves a trail of diesel fumes as it sets off. (*23 October 1989*)

A Class 91 is unusually 'blunt end' first on a special train of umber & cream Pullman stock waiting to travel south. (*25 August 1990*)

47 513 heads a parcels train in what used to be the LMS terminal station, where the six platforms were lost to parcels traffic in 1967. (*4 January 1991*)

Meanwhile across at platforms 7 & 8, the Class 141 Pacer will soon be off to Huddersfield ahead of a London departure. On a wet day, the lack of any canopy is particularly noticeable! (*4 January 1991*)

91 013 stands ready to propel to London from platform 5 beneath the old low-level roof of the 1967 train shed. Note the 'Quick Snack' café, long since gone! (*July 1990*)

Class 307s were eventually replaced by new Class 321 units, one of which heads off to Doncaster, giving a clear view of the Royal Mail liveried stock in the parcels section. (*April 1993*)

In the 1990s the view of the station from the Leeds/Liverpool Canal basin was unobstructed, and vice versa. The Hilton (ex-Drogonara) also has a clear view of both at this time. (*18 October 1992*)

After privatisation, the Cross Country services were run by Virgin, and here one of their HSTs enters Leeds from the south. (*June 1997*)

There's a station there somewhere! In total contract with the same view taken on 18 October 1992, very little of the station is revealed at all! (*6 August 2015*)

Taken thirteen years ahead of the next shot, the same scene is now totally dominated by this large cylindrical tower! (*7 August 2015*)

At the end of the total rebuild, the view into the canal basin was only partially obstructed by the canopy on the new platform 17, as a Class 156 Sprinter approaches. (*15 June 2002*)

For a time, Regional Eurostars also operated King's Cross services, and the *White Rose* set graces the rebuilt station on 31 March 2003.

Some new-build now obscures half of the Hilton, whilst a Regional Eurostar forms the 18.05 to King's Cross. (*13 July 2004*)

A reminder that the River Aire flows directly beneath the station, while a high-rise block gains elevation just south of the river/canal junction. The new southern entrance overlooks the same scene, as depicted in the next photo. (*11 April 2005*)

View from within the upper level of the new South Entrance, looking south towards the junction of the Aire and the Canal. (*5 July 2016*)

This entrance was opened on 4 January 2016. Access is gained via the car park inside the archways, and from the east & west walkways behind the nearest cross-river footbridge. Two sets of escalators then lead onto the footbridge over all the platforms, within the station. (*5 July 2016*)

The roof of the new structure extends well back over platforms 15-17 as seen here, as TransPennine set 185 135 heads west. (*5 July 2016*)

These TransPennine units (with wrap-round front windows) were introduced in 1961 on expresses between Hull and Liverpool as 6-coach trains. Still performing that role, now in blue & white livery and shorn of its buffet car, train E06 is ready to leave. (*25 July 1974*)

A 6-car rake of empty stock (four of which are of the refurbished variety) awaits permission to proceed to Neville Hill depot on a noticeably quiet day. (*15 April 1977*)

A Class 307 unit waits in the storage bay for its next turn of duty. Building work does, however, reveal a clear view straight across to the Corn Exchange's dome, at least for a time. (*July 1990*)

Another view of the same bay, this time with 307 120 sporting Metro livery, received eventually by all these units. (*25 July 1990*)

An overview of the east end, with an HST and a Class 91 offering their services. Note that the goods lines are being electrified. (*11 September 1993*)

An early morning scene, with the 06.35 HST to St Pancras soon to depart. A GNER London train and two Pacer units complete the scene on 15 August 1997.

Electrified London services have habitually used this platform, where a Class 91 in pristine GNER livery basks in the sun. (*June 1997*)

Without its name but now in full GNER livery, 89 001 also has a set of GNER-liveried coaching stock behind it. The top of the NCP car park is a useful photographic location! (*June 1997*)

For its Cross Country services, Virgin quickly replaced HSTs with new Voyager diesel units, one of which is forming the 09.07 to Newcastle from the rebuilt station, on 13 July 2004.

After the total rebuild, the east end now looks like this. The roof is of course entirely different, all tracks are now wired and the goods lines have been transformed into extra platforms. (*7 June 2005*)

The location for the previous shot was the new multi-storey car park on the left, alongside a large BT block of offices; the Hilton now has substantial red-brick buildings on either side, and another Voyager has come in. Compare this with the view taken on 11 September 1993 (*7 June 2005*)

The elevated section extends as far as Marsh Lane, and here a 2-car Class 158 unit approaches the station over the Church Walk arches on 18 October 1992. (The wires only reach Neville Hill depot.)

Back in 1985 a Class 31 heads five coaches off the elevated route and passes the remains of the old BR Marsh Lane station which closed in 1958. (*29 May 1985*)

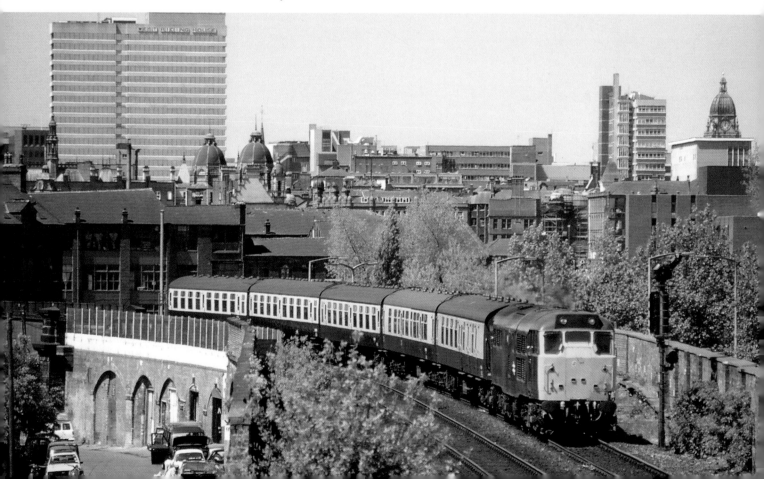

Looking east, five cars of empty stock drift down from Neville Hill, passing the site of Leeds' first station (left, here a cement-loading facility) opened in 1834 by the Leeds & Selby Railway. (*18 May 1985*)

This time looking west, a very smoky HST in 'Executive' livery makes its way to Neville Hill depot. (*21 July 1985*)

Jubilee 45596 *Bahamas* heads under the wires with the 'Scarborough Spa Express'. The large office building on the right was known locally as the 'Kremlin'. (*18 September 1994*)

Looking back through Marsh Lane cutting (it was originally a tunnel), a somewhat earlier 'Scarborough Spa Express' approaches Neville Hill behind *Evening Star*. (*29 August 1983*)

Work started in earnest in the spring of 1998 with the ex-Wellington station receiving the first attention. Here the old platform 6 is being rehabilitated, though this included retaining the 1936 LMS canopy and support columns, surprisingly. The Queens Hotel is also of 1936 LMS vintage. (*April 1998*)

The concourse of Wellington terminal station had last been in use as a car park, so required considerable refurbishment. Here are the early stages in that process. (*April 1998*)

When completed the same view looked like this, towards City Square (above) … and like this towards the platforms (below). Access to the old platforms 1–6 was gained beneath the large windows, where nowadays retail outlets abound. (*April 1998*)

The new, west-facing entrance into the north concourse forms quite an attractive façade. (*April 1998*)

Platforms 15 & 16 take shape in the space that was formerly the goods lines. (*14 July 2000*)

Platform 17 (bay platform) will appear south of platform 16, to the right of the nearest group of workers. (*14 July 2000*)

The curve of the new roof takes shape over the former Wellington platforms. (*2 October 2000*)

The new roof also rises over the southern extension, seen from the eastern end. (*3 January 2001*)

The new platform 1, utilising the LMS support columns and extended well beyond the old canopy is split into three designations, a, b & c. (*3 January 2001*)

Buffer stops at platforms 5 & 6, with contrasting trains in each. (*13 July 2001*)

158 901 enters platform 16 as work continues at the east end in the shadow of the NCP car park. (*13 July 2001*)

The Hilton overlooks progress at the west end, with platforms 13a (bay) and 17 (bay, backlit) nearing completion. (*26 October 2001*)

The Hilton also overlook the east end, where the new roof has yet to take shape, and some track renewal is still outstanding. (*13 July 2001*)

In the open west end, crowds wait on platform 4 whilst 150 268 sits happily in platform 3. (*15 April 2002*)

Work has yet to finish on the island platform 12/13/14/15, but passengers hardly notice. (*15 June 2002*)

The total rebuild was finally declared complete in 2002 on 1 August–Yorkshire day! The engineering work was recognised with an award in 2003, as illustrated here. (*7 June 2005*)

Miscellaneous relevant shots

When Wellington Street Goods Depot was still in operation, a public exhibition was staged in 1971. The KWVR provided engines 72 and 957; *The Great Marquess* (green) and 62005 also arrived, plus assorted rolling stock. The elevated approach to Central station is seen across the background. (*19 June 1971*)

After the Goods Depot had been closed and the site cleared, one of the two historic wagon hoists was chosen to remain as a reminder of the previous use of the area. It was later awarded a 'blue plaque' by the Leeds Civic Trust; see next photos. (*15 June 1985*)

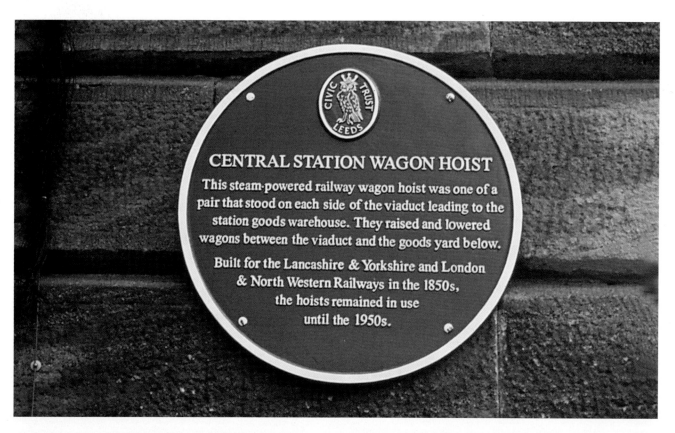

CENTRAL STATION WAGON HOIST

This steam-powered railway wagon hoist was one of a pair that stood on each side of the viaduct leading to the station goods warehouse. They raised and lowered wagons between the viaduct and the goods yard below.

Built for the Lancashire & Yorkshire and London & North Western Railways in the 1850s, the hoists remained in use until the 1950s.

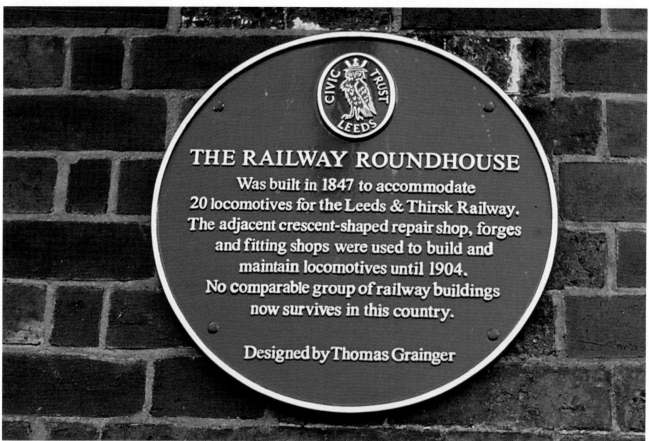

THE RAILWAY ROUNDHOUSE

Was built in 1847 to accommodate 20 locomotives for the Leeds & Thirsk Railway. The adjacent crescent-shaped repair shop, forges and fitting shops were used to build and maintain locomotives until 1904. No comparable group of railway buildings now survives in this country.

Designed by Thomas Grainger

Two self-evident Civic Trust 'blue plaques' attached to historic railway buildings. The commercial firm operating out of the Roundhouse allows an open day to be held there on an annual basis. (*August/October 2015*)

The Middleton Railway has been around since 1758, and in its 'preserved' form long had an active connection with BR. On this short stretch of connecting line (the Balm Road branch) a green saddle tank rolls a minimal train cautiously through the weeds. (*16 June 1985*)

Sir Berkeley comes off the Dartmouth branch and approaches its 'main line' on a demonstration freight, with the M621 road bridge, and associated tunnel, in the background. (*25 March 2001*)

The same engine has now reached Middleton 'top points' and will run round its train for the descent back to Moor Road. South Leeds stadium can be glimpsed on the left. (*25 March 2001*)

Map of West Yorkshire's Rail Network

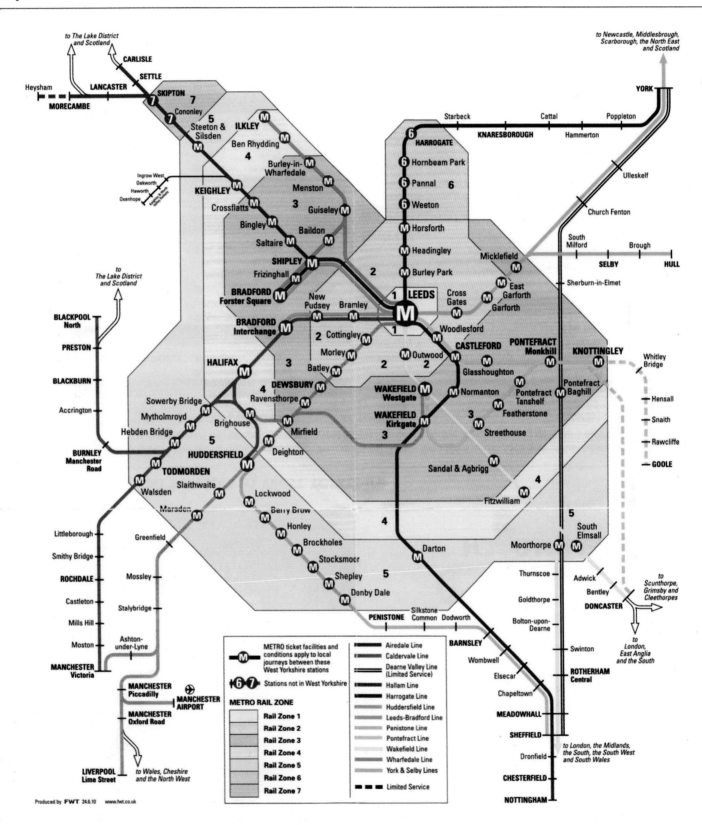

The rail zones on this map show the areas covered by West Yorkshire MetroCards and Rail Zone tickets. These season tickets offer unlimited, standard class rail travel for regular travellers within the specific zones.

The West Yorkshire Train Only, Adult Bus & Train and Family West Yorkshire DayRover tickets are only valid for travel within Zones 1 to 5. They are **not valid in Zones 6 or 7** as stations in these zones are in North Yorkshire.

Chapter Five

Metro – West Yorkshire's Rail Network
Line by Line

Examination of the current Metro map reveals a surprisingly dense local network. No less than twelve named routes appear in timetables, and sixty-seven stations are identified as Metro stations within Rail Zones 1-5 plus a further six in Zones 6 & 7 that are within North Yorkshire but served by direct trains from Leeds and/or Bradford. Of this grand total of seventy-three no fewer than twenty-three are additional stations compared with the 'since 1968' baseline, though two of these are in North Yorkshire. (It is therefore also the case that fifty of the seventy-three escaped the Beeching axe altogether, though virtually all of these have been substantially modernised since that era.) It's worth listing the twenty-three newcomers in some detail, chronologically, as below.

Name	Metro Line	Zone	Opened	Comment
1. Baildon	Wharfedale	3	05.01.1973	reopened on old site
2. Fitzwilliam	Wakefield	4	01.03.1982	reopened on old site
3. Deighton	Huddersfield	4	26.04.1982	reopened on old site
4. Crossflatts	Airedale	3	17.05.1982	new station
5. Slaithwaite	Huddersfield	5	13.12.1982	reopened on old site
6. Bramley	Calder Valley	2	12.09.1983	reopened on old site
	Leeds/Bradford			
7. Saltaire	Airedale	3	10.04.1984	reopened on old site
8. East Garforth	York & Selby	2	01.05.1987	new station
9. Frizinghall	Leeds/Bradford	3	07.09.1987	reopened on old site
	Airedale			
	Wharfedale			
10. Sandall & Agbrigg	Wakefield	3	30.11.1987	new station
11. Cononley (NY)	Airedale	7	21.04.1988	reopened on old site
12. Cottingley	Huddersfield	2	25.04.1988	new station
13. Outwood	Wakefield	2	21.07.1988	new station
14. Burley Park	Harrogate	2	29.11.1988	new station
15. Berry Brow	Penistone	5	09.10.1989	new station

Name	Metro Line	Zone	Opened	Comment
16. Steeton & Silsden	Airedale	5	14.05.1990	reopened on old site
17. Walsden	Calder Valley	5	10.09.1990	reopened on old site
18. Featherstone	Pontefract	3	11.05.1992	reopened on old site
19. Pontefract (Tanshelf)	Pontefract	3	11.05.1992	reopened on old site
20. Streethouse	Pontefract	3	11.05.1992	new station
21. Hornbeam Park (NY)	H'gate	6	24.08.1992	new station
22. Brighouse	Calder Valley	4	28.05.2000	reopened on old site
23. Glasshoughton	Pontefract	3	21.02.2005	new station

NB:

(a) 'reopened on old site' does not imply reuse of old, original buildings. All facilities are new. In some cases new platforms are staggered.

(b) 'new station' means there was not previously a station at this location.

(c) all the stations listed are unstaffed.

(d) re-nos.5 & 15; change at Huddersfield for Leeds.

(e) re-nos.18, 19, 20; change at Wakefield (Kirkgate) for Leeds.

Some of the stations listed above stretch the definition of 'around Leeds & Bradford', though all but five stations have direct trains to either city. However, for a more complete picture of the passenger developments in West Yorkshire over recent years, the author feels justified in giving this full listing. Moreover, further developments have either taken place or are in the offing and the following must also therefore be mentioned.

Name	Metro Line	Zone	Comment
X1. Leeds (Whitehall)	?	1	Open only between 1999–2002 when main station was being rebuilt. Located on the south-to-west curve of Whitehall triangle west of main station. Removed.
X2. Kirkstall Forge	Airedale	2	Opened 19 June 2016.
X3. Apperley Bridge	Airedale	2	Opened 13 December 2015.
X4. Low Moor	Calder Valley	3	Opened 2 April 2017.
X5. East Leeds Parkway	York & Selby	3	These five are proposals yet to be confirmed; all are recommended for further study.
X6. Crosshills (NY)	Airedale	7	
X7. Thorpe Park	York & Selby	3	
X8. Haxby (NY)			
X9. Elland	Calder Valley	3	
X10. Leeds (New Lane)	?	1	Proposed new separate terminus of HS2, scheduled for 2032. May be as an 'add-on' to present Leeds station.

The fact that twenty-three additional stations now enhance the Metro Network, in comparison to 1968, is indicative of the overall growth of rail usage in the Region and the active involvement of the WYPTE (and its successor WYCA), in conjunction with financial assistance from the Leeds, Bradford, Kirklees (Huddersfield), Calderdale (Halifax) and Wakefield local authorities. But how much growth? It is instructive to examine more closely the passenger numbers over the period 2004/05 to 2012/13 for some of the stations on eleven of the named Metro lines (see the following data on a line-by-line basis), and the route of the Grand Central trains.

	New Stations	2004/05	2012/13
Airedale Line (electrified 1995)	Bradford (F Sq)	404,000	2,044,000
Leeds/Bradford/Skipton	*Frizinghall* (sp) (a/c)	230,000	378,000
Northern, Virgin East Coast	Shipley	831,000	1,667,000
	Saltaire (b/c)	396,000	807,000
(sp) = staggered platforms	*Crossflatts* (a/c)	177,000	464,000
(a) heavily used by school pupils	Keighley (c)	1,088,000	1,639,000
(b) situated in World Heritage Site village	*Steeton/Silsden* (sp/c)	463,000	797,000
(c) 2013/14 figures	*Cononley* (c)	87,600	170,000
	Skipton (c)	761,000	1,002,000

Skipton is in North Yorkshire; 18¼ miles from Bradford, 26¼ miles from Leeds. *Cononley* is also in North Yorkshire.

Bradford Grammar School pupils form one of the main sources of traffic for *Frizinghall*; indeed a member of the English Department staff actively fought for its reopening, and was eventually successful. At *Saltaire*, the lower boarding point of the Shipley Glen Tramway (of 1895 vintage) is only about ten minutes walk away. *Crossflatts* station is conveniently close to Bingley Grammar School, and the Airedale line makes cross-platform interchange at Keighley with the popular Keighley & Worth Valley Railway.

The K&WVR is one of only two preserved railways which operate a complete branch line in its original form, and is now a major tourist attraction. Two years after opening, in 1970, the line received a considerable promotional boost when *The Railway Children* was shot there. Parts of the line have subsequently featured in *Yanks Go Home* (1976), *Last of the Summer Wine* (1979), *Peaky Blinders* (2013) and *Testament of Youth* (2014), amongst others. Back in June 1984 the branch was visited by a WYPTE Class 141 railbus, when a publicity film was made with a view to selling these railbuses in the export market. Later, in April 1987 two Class 150 'Sprinter' units (the first to visit a private railway) went through to Oxenhope on a K&WVR charter from Chesterfield, and later still, in November 2013 an East Midlands Trains HST (another first) ventured up the line with a charter from St Pancras. In July 2008, to celebrate the 40th anniversary of the opening, the Duke of Kent paid a visit and was provided with a 'Royal Train' consisting of steam tank engine 41241 (as per the

1968 opening) and 'The Old Gentleman's Saloon' (as per *Railway Children*). More recently, when the Tour de France passed through the Bronte Country on 6 July 2014, with local roads closed, the railway ran the most intensive timetable in its history between Keighley and Oxenhope, and 34092 *City of Wells* graced Haworth yard by displaying 'Golden Arrow' regalia to mark the cyclists' transit.

On 16 January 2011 East Coast ran a trial between Shipley and Skipton with a Class 91 loco and Mk4 coaches (to test the upgraded power supply), with a view to converting the sole Skipton–King's Cross train into an electrically hauled service after several years running as an HST unit. Skipton station had been completely renovated in 1998 prior to the introduction of this London service; and again (in a minor way) in preparation for Prince Charles's visit in 2004. The carriage sidings were upgraded in 2011 when a washing plant was also installed. Platforms 1 and 4 had been put back into use when electrification reached Skipton in 1995 together with track alterations, though platform 5 has remained in use throughout to receive freight traffic from Swinden Quarry on the Grassington branch.

At the Leeds end of the line, the stretch from Shipley into Leeds (10¾ miles) was, since 1965, one of the longest in the country to be devoid of any station on a busy commuter route. This has now changed however, with both *Apperley Bridge* and *Kirkstall Forge* opening within the last year. These two have been a long time a-coming; they were first proposed in 1999!

	New Stations	2004/05	2012/13
Wharfedale Line (electrified 1995)	Bradford (F Sq) (a)		
Leeds/Bradford/Ilkley	*Frizinghall* (a)		
Northern	Shipley (a)		
	Baildon (b)	171,000	216,000
(a) as above	Guiseley	628,000	1,135,000
(b) closed 05.01.1953	Menston	330,000	578,000
reopened 28.01.1957	Ilkley	810,000	1,212,000
closed 29.04.1957			
reopened 05.01.1973 exactly 20 years after initial closure; now on single track.			

Ilkley is 13¾ miles from Bradford, 16½ miles from Leeds. Only terminus-to-terminus working of the Metro services.

Baildon was the first station to reopen post-1968. One of the original platforms is still used; the main station building remains intact, though not for railway purposes.

After a decade of uncertainty, in 1987 work started on a £3.6 million plan to redevelop Ilkley station to include a shopping centre and a new bus terminus. (Ilkley was the last BR station to be lit by gas; the lights were extinguished for the final time on 8 May 1988.) It was also later refurbished with new buildings, ticket office, waiting rooms and shelters, CCTV and better PA system, this work being completed in November 2011. Guiseley's facilities were also enhanced in

2002 with new waiting rooms on both platforms, and a replacement ticket office. Menston was also considerably redeveloped in 2000; the station building has been refurbished and now contains a ticket office displaying the Ian Allan National Railway Heritage Award plaque for 2000, presented by Sir Alastair Morton, Chairman Strategic Rail Authority. Just outside a bus service gives connections to Otley and Leeds/Bradford airport. The ceremonial opening of electric services from Ilkley to Leeds took place on 25 May 1995; public services began on the 28th with the summer timetable.

(It would be helpful to Wharfedale Line commuters if Virgin could be persuaded that one of their early morning Leeds – London services could start back at Ilkley (and call at Kirkstall Forge). This would also spread the track access charges on the Wharfedale Line. After all, Virgin already start King's Cross trains at Skipton, Bradford Forster Square and Harrogate; Ilkley seems to be the odd one out!)

	New Stations	2004/05	2012/13
Harrogate Line	Leeds (a)	18,121,000	27,729,000
Leeds/Harrogate	*Burley Park* (c)	327,000	588,000
Northern, Virgin East Coast	Headingley	164,000	337,000
	Horsforth	615,000	960,000
(a) 2007/08 to 2013/14	*Hornbeam P'k* (sp/c)	209,000	303,000
(sp) = staggered platforms	Harrogate	1,055,000	1,361,000
(c) 2013/14 figures			

Harrogate is 18¼ miles north of Leeds.

Both *Hornbeam Park* and Harrogate are in North Yorkshire. Many services from Leeds continue to Knaresborough and York. The Virgin train to King's Cross from Harrogate in the early morning is an HST unit, calling at Horsforth southbound only, Mon-Fri.

Burley Park was opened by the Lord Mayor of Leeds and is situated close to Headingley Stadium, for rugby and cricket matches. It has no attached car park. The TV series *Emmerdale* occasionally uses *Burley Park* in the role of Hotton station. Headingley is also close to the Stadium, and to Leeds University's Beckett Park campus. Horsforth (5¾ miles from Leeds station and where cheap fares end!) was extensively redeveloped in 2002/3 with new waiting rooms, ticket office and extended car park. *Hornbeam Park* is only one mile south of Harrogate (and at £413,000 very expensive for a 2-platform halt!?).

In 2011 Harrogate Chamber of Commerce put forward the strange idea of electrifying the entire York/Harrogate/Leeds route at 750V DC using redundant 'D' stock from London Underground's District Line, with 3rd rail side-contact conductor-rail pick-up. The proposal actually got as far as the Transport Minister, though fortunately it was kicked into touch by Metro, Northern Rail and National Rail as it was estimated to cost £150 million, and both York and Leeds were already using the 25kV AC overhead system!

	New Stations	2004/05	2012/13
York & Selby Line	Leeds (a)		
Leeds/Micklefield	Cross Gates	239,000	454,000
Northern, TransPennine and Cross Country	Garforth	440,000	611,000
	East Garforth (c)	157,000	223,000
	Micklefield (sp)	123,000	179,000
(a) as above (c) 2013/14 figures			
(sp) = staggered platforms			

Micklefield is 9¾ miles east of Leeds.

Only about 2½ miles east of Leeds station is situated the extensive diesel and electric maintenance depot at Neville Hill. The site has been in railway use ever since the North Eastern Railway opened a shed here in the 1890s and enlarged it to its current extent in 1904; it finally closed to BR steam in 1966. The original buildings were either demolished, or refurbished and modernised, and further buildings were added to the site in 1960 (two) and 1979. It was electrified in April 1990 and is home base to a large allocation of Class 321, 322 & 333 e.m.u.s and Leeds-area d.m.u.s, and also services a wide variety of Northern's Pacers and Sprinters, HST units of East Midlands Trains and East Coast coaching stock – one of the major depots in the North of England. On 13 September 2009 Northern Rail organised a 'Community Day' here, when the depot was open to the public for the first time in thirty-six years, apparently; the displays included preserved steam engines and 'heritage' diesel locos, a naming ceremony for HST Power car 43 082 as *Railway Children* as well as multiple trade stands. All proceeds (over £7,000) were donated to charity. Cross Gates was the former junction for the line to Wetherby, closed in 1964; Garforth was the former junction for Castleford, closed in 1969. East Garforth serves new housing development. Micklefield is the last West Yorkshire station before the lines to York and to Selby split just east of the station, and enter North Yorkshire.

	New Stations	2004/05	2012/13
Pontefract Line	Leeds (a)		
Leeds/Knottingley	Woodlesford (sp)	156,000	292,000
Northern, Grand Central	Castleford	293,000	538,000
	Glasshoughton (b)	2,104	180,000
(a) as above	Pontefract (Monkhill)	113,000	231,000
(b) only opened 21.02.2005	Knottingley	85,416	141,000
(h) see Hallam Line comment	*Pontefract (Tanshelf)*	24,690	39,580
(sp) = staggered platforms	*Featherstone* (sp)	52,530	81,452
	Streethouse	23,492	30,746
	Wakefield (Kirkgate)	(h) 372	508,000

Knottingley is 16 miles south-east of Leeds.

All Grand Central trains call at Wakefield (K), some also stop at Monkhill. Passenger trains between Monkhill and Kirkgate were withdrawn on 2 January 1967, the line remaining freight only until 12 May 1992 when the three new stations restored passenger services.

Except for X2, X3 and X4, *Glasshoughton* is the most recent addition to the Metro network. Built at a cost of £2.3 million (mainly due to the large boundary stone wall) the station serves the Xscape ski & leisure complex and the Freeport shopping centre; a 100 space car park adjoins the station. Being on the edge of the Metro network, most trains either start from, or terminate at Knottingley, though the line goes through to Goole (North Yorkshire). *Tanshelf* is close to Pontefract racecourse. During the summers, steam-hauled excursions have been frequent visitors to Kirkgate on their way to Scarborough.

	New Stations	2004/05	2012/13
Wakefield Line (electrified 1989)	Leeds (a)		
Leeds/South Elmsall/Moorthorpe	*Outwood* (c)	166,000	349,000
	W'field (Westgate)	1,760,000	2,358,000
Northern, Virgin East Coast, East Midlands Trains and Cross Country	*Sandal & Agbrigg* (c)	97,328	260,000
	Fitzwilliam (c)	105,000	256,000
	South Elmsall (b)	253,000	357,000
(a) as above (c) 2013/14 figures	Moorthorpe (b)	146,000	227,000
(b) SYPTE tickets also valid	Doncaster	2,903,000	3,835,000

Doncaster is in South Yorkshire, 29¾ miles south-east of Leeds.

Westgate was, for twenty years from 1988, noted for its piece of public art on platform 2 – a modern sculpture 'A Light Wave' by a Leeds-based artist. In wood, and illuminated from behind at night, the weather eventually took its toll and the 'planks in the form of waves against a wall' were removed in 2009. Considerable regeneration work has taken place on the site of the old goods yard north-east of the station in recent years, 2007-2010. Work began transforming the station itself in March 2013 and it was ready for use on 22 December, with an official opening by the Transport Minister on 3 February 2014. New footbridge, travel centre, lounges and waiting rooms, retail outlets and ticket gates all feature in the rebuild. Westgate appears in the TV series *A Touch of Frost* in the role of Denton Station.

Sandal & Agbrigg's opening on 30 November 1987 was celebrated by 140 local schoolchildren taking a 'Santa special' trip into Leeds. Moorthorpe was reduced to the status of an un-manned halt in the 1970s, with the station converted into a pub – 'The Mallard'. This closed in the 1990s and became derelict, but has happily been restored by the town council and now contains offices, community café and booking hall. In 2010 a new footbridge replaced the previous flat crossing of the tracks. The Dearne Valley line from York joins the Wakefield line immediately north of this station.

	New Stations	2004/05	2012/13
Dearne Valley Line	York	5,796,000	8,223,000
York/Sheffield	Pontefract (Baghill)	53	5,252
Northern	Moorthorpe (a)	146,000	227,000
(a) also on Wakefield line	Sheffield	7, 334,000	8,615,000

Pontefract (Baghill) is 21¼ miles south of York. Sheffield is in South Yorkshire, approximately 40 miles south of Leeds; first figure relates to 2008/09. York's second figure is for 2013/14.

Only two trains per day stop at Baghill in each direction. In 2002/03 the Strategic Rail Authority's figures showed only thirty-six people used the station, making it the sixth least busy station in the UK. However, the SRA has difficulty in allocating passenger numbers for stations that are grouped together, as tickets are booked to 'Pontefract Stations' and not to a particular station, hence adjusted figures can be wrong either way. Baghill's allocated figure for 2006/07 was 64,802 – which may well have been the total for all three of Pontefract's stations! The 2012/13 figure is probably reliable.

	New Stations	2004/05	2012/13
Hallam Line	Leeds (a)		
Leeds/Sheffield	Woodlesford (sp)	156,000	292,000
Northern	Castleford	293,000	538,000
	Normanton	113,000	245,000
(a) as above	W'field (Kirkgate)	372	508,000
(sp) = staggered platforms	Darton (b)	134,000	202,000

(b) Darton is in South Yorkshire, 21½ miles south of Leeds but WYPTE tickets are valid to and from this station.

Soon after leaving Leeds, the former Holbeck depot is passed on the right. Once a major steam shed, the last loco (45428) left under its own power on 24 August 1968. Just a couple of miles south of Leeds, the Midland Road Depot of Freightliner Maintenance Ltd is passed on the east side of the line. This Depot was opened on 11 July 2003 and services Class 66 locomotives and wagons for that company. Only a mile or so further on, this time on the west side, is Stourton Freightliner Terminal for container traffic, in action since June 1967. At Woodlesford, the pedestrian crossing between the staggered platforms was replaced by a footbridge in 2010. All services reverse direction at Castleford, where the new bus station was hoped to adjoin the railway station; this plan fell through. After Castleford, Wakefield Europort can be seen between the line and the M62 motorway. This facility was opened in 1996 to cater mainly for international freight traffic coming through the Channel Tunnel, though very little of this materialised. By 2009 the site was working at about half capacity, and only for inter-modal transfers. As of 2011, the railport was operated by DB Schenker Rail (UK), successor to English, Welsh & Scottish Railway (EWS). In Victorian times Normanton was one of the most important stations in the north of England, being served by three of the early companies, thereby accessing much of the country. Queen Victoria even stopped overnight at the Station Hotel! Much diminished nowadays, the pedestrian crossing at the end of platform 2 has recently been replaced by a footbridge.

In 2009 Kirkgate was described as 'the worst medium/large station in Britain' by the Secretary of State for Transport Lord Adonis. Since then, regeneration work has enhanced the station considerably though it remains unstaffed and further work has now been completed. As most tickets were, in 2004/05, bought to 'Wakefield Stations' it was difficult to determine the true use of Westgate and Kirkgate as separate entities. Beginning in 2007/08, changes in methodology have increased the reliability of the statistics; the latest totals should therefore be regarded as reasonably accurate. (The three stations at Pontefract were similarly 'grouped'.)

	New Stations	2004/05	2012/13
Penistone Line	Huddersfield	2,214,000	4,657,000
Huddersfield/Sheffield	*Berry Brow*	19,572	25,978
Northern	Denby Dale	75,853	177,000
single track throughout	Penistone (a)	107,000	122,000
(a) 2004/05 to 2010/11			

Penistone is in South Yorkshire, 19½ miles from Huddersfield.

Berry Brow was opened by the Chairman of the WYPTA attended by a jazz band; a class from the local Infants & Nursery School got a free train ride to Huddersfield and back. Denby Dale is 9½ miles south of Huddersfield; both Metro and South Yorkshire tickets are valid to and from this unstaffed boundary station. There are passing loops between Stocksmoor and Shepley, and at Penistone. South of here, the line is double track through Barnsley to Sheffield.

Denby Dale has a long tradition of baking giant pies! The first was baked in 1788 to celebrate George III's recovery from his mental illness, and the most recent – the ninth – to celebrate the millenium in 2000. This one weighed a whopping 12 tonnes! As can be inferred from the dates, these 'Pie Festivals' are not frequent occurrences; when the previous one was baked in 1964, ten extra trains ran from Huddersfield – all full!

The 3½ mile branch from Shepley to Clayton West survived the Beeching closures, but was not subsequently supported by the WYPTE and was closed on 24 January 1983, becoming the second last 'significant' closure in England before the re-openings of the late 1980s (the last being Eridge/Tunbridge Wells). The trackbed is now occupied almost in its entirety by the 15 in. gauge Kirklees Light Railway which opened on 19 October 1991 by running from Clayton West to a new halt at Cuckoos Nest (1 mile). The line was extended to Skelmanthorpe in 1992 (in the shadow of the Emley Moor TV transmitter) and reached its current terminus at Shelley in May 1997. Total length is now 3¾ miles and includes passage through Shelley Woodhouse Tunnel, at 511yd. the longest on any 15 in. gauge line in Britain. The four steam locos were all built by the original owner over the period 1987 – 2000; these are based on old designs but with some advanced features for ease of operation nowadays. The line changed hands in 2006 on the owners' retirement, but thrives as 'Yorkshire's Great Little Steam Train', and on gala weekends attracts visiting 15 in. gauge locos as well!

After several years of doubts, the 'main' line was only made 'secure' when the freight line from Penistone to Barnsley was upgraded and services diverted via this route as from 16 May 1983. Formed in 1993, the Penistone Line Partnership has since worked tirelessly to raise the profile of the line through the running of folk music trains, jazz trains, beer trains, dedicated bus feeders and publicity. Despite the success of these efforts, Network Rail seriously suggested (in 2008) that a two-year trial take place running 'tram-trains' over this route, all the way to Sheffield. However, the line north of Penistone alone contains seven tunnels and five viaducts whose maintenance costs would hardly change, and almost all of the seventeen stations *en route* would require their platforms lowering. These costs, plus the expenditure on the new vehicles themselves, would not be recouped by the lower running and maintenance costs of the tram-trains themselves, especially as seating capacity would actually be reduced – hardly conducive to increased fare-box revenue! The scheme was not pursued, and the line continues to thrive in 'heavy-rail' form. 'Tram-trains' are now running trials between Meadowhall and Parkgate in South Yorkshire.

	New Stations	2004/05	2012/13
Huddersfield Line	Leeds (a)		
Leeds/Marsden	*Cottingley* (c)	25,179	102,770
Northern, TransPennine	Dewsbury	743,000	1,604,000
	Deighton (c)	25,636	95,000
(a) as above (c) 2013/14 figures	Huddersfield	2,214,000	4,657,000
(b) single early morning train through to Leeds, otherwise change at Huddersfield.	*Slaithwaite* (b/c) (sp)	99,000	208,000
	Marsden (b)	100,000	167,000
(sp) = staggered platforms			

Marsden is 24 miles south-west of Leeds, but only 19 miles from Manchester. *Slaithwaite* is exactly half-way between Leeds and Manchester. At least some of the traffic from these two stations (and Huddersfield) will be heading west! Marsden is unusual in having three platforms, each accessed separately. This station is only ½ mile from the Standedge rail and canal tunnels.

Both *Cottingley* and *Deighton* have exhibited huge increases in patronage in the last nine years; indeed the line has seen healthy growth throughout its length at least partly due to congestion on the M62. However, overcrowding on this rail route is severe into Leeds during the peak periods, despite a frequent service.

Huddersfield station is a Grade I listed building, with a classical façade, the frontage being described as 'one of the best early railway stations in England'. It has six platforms, numbered 1-8 with nos. 3 and 7 absent! In both 2010 and 2011 many improvements were made, including two new lifts and a new staircase, plus new information screens. Additionally ticket barriers were installed in 2013 and upgraded in 2014 to accept smartcards, as do those at Leeds and Bradford Interchange.

On 10 August 2003 the Penistone Line Partnership celebrated their 10th birthday by organising a Huddersfield Station Gala with diesel and steam locos on display, and cab rides

for children out to Lockwood and back. Pacer unit 144 001 was also named *Penistone Line Partnership*. A similar event took place on 13 May 2007 – again run by the PLP – to mark Community Rail Week. Both diesel and steam locos were present and once more roughly 2,000 people attended. The Department for Transport announced in 2008 that trials of 'tram-trains' were to take place on the Huddersfield/Penistone/Sheffield line during 2010/11. This proposal collapsed, see Penistone line comments above.

	New Stations	2004/05	2012/13
Calder Valley Line	Leeds (a)		
Leeds/Walsden	*Bramley* (sp) (c)	137,000	317,000
Northern, Grand Central	New Pudsey (c)	424,000	764,000
	B'ford (Inter) (b)	2,401,000	2,990,000
(a) as above (c) 2013/14 figures	Halifax (c)	940,000	1,913,000
(b) to 2013/14; reverse here	Todmorden	297,000	542,000
(d) only new station to show	*Walsden* (c) (d)	126,000	94,000
a decrease in usage			
(sp) = staggered platforms			

Walsden is 32¼ miles west of Leeds; 17¾ miles east of Manchester (Victoria)!

In its early days (1969) New Pudsey featured in a Monty Python sketch! Initially the long platforms provided here served through trains from Bradford Exchange/Interchange to King's Cross, though when the ECML was electrified and the London trains diverted to Forster Square, this function became redundant.

Following the re-instatement of the relevant junctions in 2000, Halifax was again able to offer westbound trains to Brighouse and Huddersfield, as well as the regular Manchester services. Due largely to vociferous local pressure regarding the disgraceful state of Halifax station, a £2.5 million

refurbishment scheme was initiated here in May 2009 and completed in November 2010. From 23 May 2010 Halifax was again connected directly to King's Cross when Grand Central began operating via *Brighouse* (see below). Previous direct services to London, via Huddersfield and Wakefield (Westgate) had ceased in the 1970s.

At Todmorden the Manchester/Burnley chord has been re-instated as from May 2015 and services now run through from Blackburn, Accrington and Burnley into Manchester via the Calder Valley for the first time in forty years. Platform 1 here contains an art gallery open four days a week, alongside the ticket office and waiting room.

The decline in Walsden's passenger numbers is not particularly significant; *Berry Brow* is regarded as successful with only 26,000! Perhaps the fact that most of the hourly trains to/from Leeds and Manchester now run via Brighouse rather than Bradford and Halifax has something to do with this. After Walsden the line passes under the Pennines at Summit Tunnel, the scene of the serious fire in 1984 that closed the line for some eight months.

There have been several proposals to open a replacement station at *Low Moor* (3 miles south of Bradford) ever since 1994. Finally however, this new station opened on 2 April 2017. Between July 1995 and October 1997, the site of Low Moor station and part of the trackbed towards Cleckheaton was home to 'Transperience'. This museum of passenger transport featured a ride on a Hungarian tram, or on a trolleybus, amongst other attractions, but visitor numbers were disappointing and the facility was very short-lived. Most of the site is now an industrial estate.

	New Stations	2004/05	2012/13
Grand Central Railway Route	B'ford (Inter) (c)	2,401,000	2,990,000
Bradford (Interchange) to King's Cross service	Halifax (c)	940,000	1,913,000
	Brighouse (c)	64,000	372,000
(c) 2013/14 figures	Mirfield (sp)	134,000	393,000
(d) from 2007/08	W'field (Kirkgate) (d)	360,000	508,000
(sp) = staggered platforms	Pontefract (Monkhill)	113,000	231,000

Open access operator Grand Central commenced running out of Bradford Interchange on 23 May 2010, initially with three trains per day but with four as from December 2013, and has operating rights until the end of 2026. The extra stop at Mirfield was inserted in December 2011. After Pontefract services call at Doncaster, then non-stop to London. In February 2015 Grand Central gained the highest customer score (76 per cent) in *Which?* magazine's 'Best and Worst Train Companies' survey!

Having been closed for thirty years *Brighouse* was reopened on 27 May 2000 as part of a gala day festival when the Halifax/Huddersfield link was restored after fifteen years of disuse. Declared open by the Calder Valley MP, normal timetabled services began the following day. It had originally been the intention to open a new station at Elland at the same time, but lack of funds prevented this (though looking at the substantial growth in passenger numbers since, Elland would probably be successful as well!).

Mirfield, unusually, has three platforms; numbers 1 & 2 form an island platform but the third was added in the 1980s to increase capacity and is staggered with respect to the others. The station had an overall roof until this was demolished in 1977.

Between Mirfield and Wakefield the train passes the site of the former Healey Mills Marshalling Yard. Opened in 1963 as part of BR's plan to modernise the sorting of wagon-load traffic, this hump shunting yard covered 140 acres and had a capacity of over 4,000 wagons per day – exceeded in busy times. A diesel maintenance depot was opened on the site in late 1966 and had its own loco allocation, many of which were employed in moving coal trains. By the mid-1980s much of this traffic (about 50 per cent of the total) had vanished, most of the sidings were out of use, and Healey Mills closed for revenue-earning traffic in November 1989. After which many withdrawn locos were stored here pending scrapping, and following privatisation the depot was used only as a staff signing-on point for crew changes of passing freight trains. DB Schenker finally closed its staff depot here in March 2012, marking the end of all operations at the site, once one of the largest marshalling yards in Britain. Remarkably it has an unusual claim to fame for a freight facility in that the Queen once slept overnight in the yard aboard the Royal Train during her 1977 Silver Jubilee tour of the country!

Further east, between Wakefield (Kirkgate) and Pontefract (Monkhill), the Grand Central service passes its own maintenance depot at Crofton, opened on 27 February 2001 by Bombardier. Beyond Pontefract the former diesel depot at Knottingley is also passed. This was built by BR in the 1960s, but lost its allocation of locos in 1987. Its function nowadays is largely confined to wagon repairs.

Considering the downturn in the economy for several years after the banking crisis of 2008, the above figures are impressive official estimates of passenger usage based on sales of tickets which either originated at, or terminated at, each of the stations. Of the top ten busiest new stations it is noticeable that seven are on electrified lines.

It is also worthwhile separating out from the above information the top ten busiest stations (in terms of passenger usage) in two categories, and identifying the relevant percentage increases.

Established stations; % increase in usage since 2004/05

	2012/2013	2013/2014	%
Leeds (since 2007/08)		27,729,000	53.0
Huddersfield	4,657,000		85.5
Bradford (Interchange)		2,990,000	24.5
Wakefield (Westgate)		2,358,000	33.0
Bradford (Forster Square)		2,044,000	405.9
Halifax		1,913,000	103.5
Shipley	1,667,000		100.6
Keighley		1,639,000	50.6
Dewsbury	1,604,000		115.9
Ilkley	1,212,000		49.6
NY Harrogate	1,361,000		29.0
NY Skipton		1,002,000	53.0
SY Doncaster (2007/08)	3,835,000		32.1

New stations; % increase in usage since 2004/05

		2013/2014	%
Saltaire	(electrified)	807,000	103.8
Steeton & Silsden	(electrified)	797,000	72.1
Burley Park		588,000	79.8
Crossflatts	(electrified)	464,000	162.1
Frizinghall	(electrified)	378,000	64.3
Brighouse		372,000	481.3
Outwood	(electrified)	349,000	110.2
Bramley		317,000	131.4
Sandal & Agbrigg	(electrified)	260,000	168.0
Fitzwilliam	(electrified)	256,000	143.8
NY *Hornbeam Park*		303,000	45.0

Of the twelve named lines listed on the Metro Map only four are currently electrified, yet seven of the ten new (West Yorkshire) stations tabulated above are on three of these. Looking at the list of the top ten busiest established stations, only four are not on electrified lines – two on the Huddersfield line and two on the Calder Valley line. As the first of these is proposed for electrification (as part of the 'Northern Hub', now delayed), it seems likely that a large increase in passenger numbers would follow.

The proposed stations X5–X9 listed above emerged from a Feasibility Study of possible sites for new stations in North and West Yorkshire. This large Report examined over sixty potential locations in these regions, but short-listed only five. Considerations of likely demand, construction difficulty and line capacity ruled out the vast majority at this time, though *if* the 'Northern Hub' project comes to fruition the groundwork has been done for others amongst the sixty-plus to be revisited at short notice.

Interestingly, no less than eleven stations within the Metro area appear on Network Rail's lengthy list of those stations with 'listed building' status. Top of the list is, of course, Huddersfield (Grade I), but ten others fall into the Grade II category, though the author is suspicious that it may no longer be correct in certain cases! Following the order of lines detailed above, the ten are:

Keighley	(built 1883, listed 1986)	Airedale Line
Skipton	(built 1886, listed 1991)	Airedale Line
Ilkley	(built 1865, listed 1976)	Wharfedale Line
Headingley	(built 1847, listed 1999)	Harrogate Line
Wakefield (Kirkgate)	(built 1857, listed 1979)	Wakefield Line
Ravensthorpe	(built 1891, listed 1988)	Huddersfield Line
Dewsbury	(built 1889, listed 1991)	Huddersfield Line
Halifax	(built 1885, listed 1990)	Calder Valley Line
Mytholmroyd	(built 1847, listed 1984)	Calder Valley Line
Hebden Bridge	(built 1906, listed 1978)	Calder Valley Line.

Early days at Frizinghall. The northbound platform is intact, but little else in the way of facilities exists, as a 3-car Class 144 Pacer approaches from Shipley. The station had been open since Sept 1987. (*7 May 1988*)

This unit then stops at the staggered southbound platform which looks rather more complete. (*7 May 1988*)

Nowadays the longer Bradford-bound platform looks rather different! Better waiting shelter, information screens and a full car park are all partially protected by mature trees. And the line is electrified. (*4 August 2015*)

A busy platform 1 sees a Class 322 loading up as a Class 333 slows to a stop a few yards further on. (*4 August 2015*)

Viewed through the connecting road bridge, the 333 makes its last call before Forster Square. As far as possible, WYPTE's new stations used existing bridges to connect the two platforms, even if this meant staggering these. (*4 August 2015*)

Between Shipley and Saltaire, the large 'Salts' mill dominates the trackside, especially when recently stone-cleaned! The train is the Carlisle/Nottingham, heading for Leeds. (*5 April 1980*)

Taken from the window of the excellent café within the mill, *Duchess of Hamilton* accelerates a special towards Saltaire. (*11 August 1993*)

Saltaire's original station had closed ten years earlier as 1S68, the former *Thames-Clyde Express*, passes through the site. (*28 May 1975*)

Now reopened for more than a year, the stone-clad shelters were provided to match the surrounding village. A Bradford/Keighley local d.m.u. service draws to a halt past look-alike gas lamps; the road bridge serves to connect the platforms. (*9 June 1985*)

Trackwork in preparation for electrification brought several ballast trains to the area. Here a Class 47 stands in Saltaire station, waiting to draw forward to the required spot. (*26 April 1992*)

A modern-day shot from the same position, with a Bradford train about to depart amongst the foliage. Saltaire had been declared a UNESCO World Heritage Site in December 2001. (*3 August 2015*)

This train having left, the mill, its chimney and canteen (behind the shelter) are then clearly seen. (*3 August 2015*)

Only a short walk from the station is another 'rail' attraction. Operating since 1895 and often under threat of closure, the Glen Tramway is now owned by Bradford Council, but run by a Charitable Trust with a 125 year lease. So hopefully it's safe. (*26 March 2001*)

This is the site of the future Crossflatts station just north of Bingley, being passed by the northbound *Thames-Clyde Express*. (*November 1974*)

Nearly a year after opening, the rudimentary wooden platform hosts a Keighley-bound service from Bradford. (*26 March 1983*)

The updated station now hosts updated trains; an e.m.u. for Skipton pulls in. (*4 August 2015*)

A lengthy ramp leads to the road overbridge, and the Bingley bypass now carries traffic noisily below, and to the right of, this ramp. (*4 August 2015*)

Apart from electric lighting, in the early 1970s Keighley had seen little change for many years. (*3 June 1972*)

By 1978 the platform canopies had gone as *Evening Star* arrives with the special train to Appleby to unveil the plaque in memory of Bishop Eric Treacy, who died on the station platform there. (*30 September 1978*)

By the mid-1980s, first generation d.m.u.s running the Metro services were in their old age and in need of replacement. A typical pair occupy both platforms 1 & 2; the KWVR platforms are behind the 'Keighley' platform sign. (*8 August 1985*)

The d.m.u.'s replacements had, in fact, already been retired! When photographed, this Class 308 was 36 years old, though looking smart in its Metro livery on a Skipton/Bradford service. (*November 1997*)

The KWVR attracts many specials from far afield, and here *Union of South Africa* is arriving from Edinburgh. 43924 and *City of Wells* will haul the train up the valley, 60009 will go on to York, and the Class 47 will return the excursion to Scotland. (*14 September 1985*)

Three years later, the right-hand side has been totally redeveloped and a Sainsbury store has arrived on the left, while a Skipton/Leeds d.m.u. slows for the stop. (*27 February 1988*)

'The North Yorkshireman' steam special runs through behind *Flying Scotsman*. (This had started from Forster Square – see that section). The Midland Railway Goods depot and coal yard are still intact, and Keighley station entrance straddles the road bridge in the background. (*23 June 1981*)

Eight years forward, and Sainsbury's store and car park now occupy the right and Peter Black the left. In between *The Great Marquess* heads north, having just come on to power a special from King's Cross largely composed of Pullman stock. (*9 July 1989*)

At Steeton & Silsden a large car park adjoins the northbound platform, always busy as this is the last station in West Yorkshire – subsidised fares end here! (*4 August 2015*)

Unusually, the platforms are both staggered and overlap. On the left the original Midland Railway station buildings survive in private hands. (*4 August 2015*)

Cononley (North Yorkshire) has two platforms connected, this time, by a level crossing over a local road which a train for Skipton is passing over on 4 August 2015.

Skipton – before things changed. Everything looks to be still in the steam age, with signal box, semaphores and even a steam engine, *Green Arrow* about to take over an incoming special. However, a Class 144 Pacer can be spotted in the platform, and another on the extreme left in the siding. (*5 June 1991*)

Just a few weeks before the services were electrified, Pacer 144 012 in Regional Railways livery stands beneath the wires. (This unit was later to become the 'Evolution Pacer' rebuilt by Porterbrook in 2015). The station has been refurbished ahead of hosting the second-hand e.m.u.s, some 25 years older than the Pacers! (*22 April 1995*)

Twenty years later the current station is well-kept and really quite attractive. It would also be a lot busier if North Yorkshire decided to subsidise its train services! (*4 August 2015*)

Only Skipton had the siding space to store electric units, and a washing plant was therefore installed here as well. (*4 August 2015*)

At the Leeds end of the line, the new Apperley Bridge is seen here under construction. The train is heading west past the incomplete Leeds-bound platform. (*7 August 2015*)

This is the staggered west-bound platform at Apperley Bridge, to be approached from a car park on the right. (*7 August 2015*)

Still not open, the station now advertises itself from the main road. (*25 October 2015*)

Apperley Bridge was finally opened on 13 December 2015, and a Class 333 halts with a service for Leeds on 5 July 2016.

Another Class 333 runs into the westbound platform 2. The large adjacent car park (on a slightly higher level) is reached from this side via steps or a zig-zag ramp. A small, existing road bridge (now pedestrian-only) gives access to the platforms. (*5 July 2016*)

The 15.49 service to Bradford Forster Square is provided by Class 322 (built by BREL at York, 1990). (*5 July 2016*)

The most recent additional station was Kirkstall Forge, opened on 19 June 2016, and a Class 333 is seen rushing through towards Leeds. (*5 July 2016*)

Here, a footbridge with lifts connects the two platforms, and ramps from the pedestrian-only south side entrance (close to the Leeds–Liverpool Canal) lead directly onto platform 2. The station will ultimately serve a development with 1000 houses, office space and retail outlets plus a large car park. (*5 July 2016*)

Wharfedale Line

The only station to reopen in West Riding days was Baildon; all the rest have been under the auspices of West Yorkshire. (*20 February 1973*)

Adjacent posters; on the left fifteen lines are shown, as the West Riding then included Sheffield and Doncaster. (*20 February 1973*)

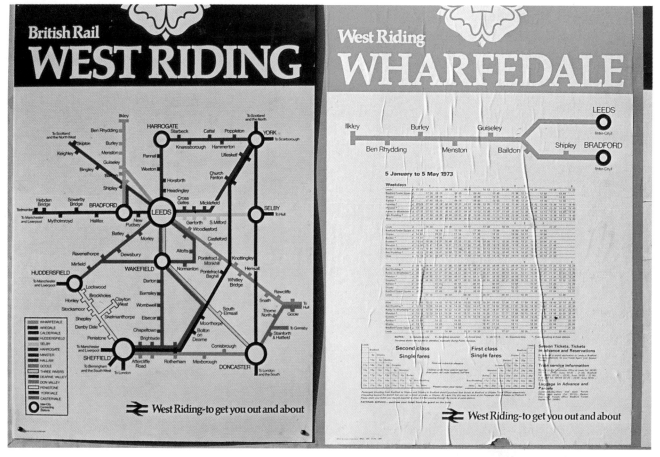

The Ilkley-bound platform. Note the new steps onto the road bridge used to connect the platforms at this time. (*20 February 1973*)

Recent view from the road bridge; the line between Guiseley Junction at Shipley, and Guiseley station was singled years ago and the second platform removed. (*4 August 2015*)

The 11.56 to Ilkley pulling out. Baildon is one of only two new stations to be on single track. (*4 August 2015*)

Guiseley station prior to the substantial alterations made later when the stone buildings on the left were taken down and the signal box removed. A Met-Camm d.m.u. departs towards Ilkley. (*29 August 1972*)

A basic shelter now adorns platform 1 as a special HST working heads for Ilkley. (*21 January 1989*)

Platform 1 now looks very different – and much improved! (*4 August 2015*)

The Leeds/Bradford platform is also decidedly more customer friendly. (*4 August 2015*)

The line onwards from Ilkley to Skipton did not escape closure, and these trains used to run through from platforms 3 & 4, labelled in this shot, but defunct. Platform 1 has the 11.25 to Bradford. (*1 February 1969*)

Now rationalised and refurbished, 144 002 handles Leeds traffic in No.1, whilst 144 001 waits as the next Bradford service. (*April 1993*)

Forced to embark in the open as the buffer stops have been repositioned (!), the ancient e.m.u. is the Leeds train, as the newer Pacer looks on. Milepost 211¼ is 'from St. Pancras'. (*6 May 1995*)

Perhaps surprisingly, the canopies for the Skipton platforms still exist, where now cars happily park. (*4 August 2015*)

Since 2001, Class 333 units now form the regular services to both Leeds and Bradford, an immense improvement! (*4 August 2015*)

The recently installed cycle racks are also proving popular, though a sunny day helps. (*4 August 2015*)

Part of Armley viaduct is seen on the right as 2 x 2-car Class 141 Pacers in 'Verona green & buttermilk' Metro livery head for Harrogate on 6 August 1985.

First station out of Leeds is now Burley Park, where a Class 150 + 153 pairing forms one of the hourly trains to Knaresborough. Again a local road bridge provides the platform connection. (*3 August 2015*)

Horsforth is the last Metro station on this line, and *Clan Line* with full 'Golden Arrow' regalia is an unlikely sight passing through on a York/York circular railtour. (*26 August 1979*)

Close-in to Harrogate, North Yorkshire have provided a new station at Hornbeam Park, with staggered platforms separated by a road overbridge. No. 1 is the Leeds platform. (*4 August 2015*)

No. 2 is the northbound platform, seen through the bridge as a Leeds train approaches. (*4 August 2015*)

Part of Harrogate station was, on 21 September 1975, given over to an exhibition advertising shirts! Quite why I cannot remember, but preserved Midland compound 1000 brought in the special coaching stock, an attraction in itself.

Neville Hill Open Day 29 April 1973 sees a variety of rolling stock ranged around one of the turntables in the old steam shed, before everything was demolished. Thirty-six years later a similar event took place, though in a very different, thoroughly modern depot!

East Garforth is one of the few stations where a new footbridge has had to be constructed to access both platforms. Here a train for Leeds enters No.2 formed by a 3-car set (Classes 153 + 150 units). (*3 August 2015*)

An overview from the footbridge as a Class 185 TransPennine 3-car set rushes through towards Leeds. (*3 August 2015*)

Micklefield is the most easterly station on this line, where a Class 31 is seen passing through from Leeds with mineral wagons. (*23 March 1989*)

Before it closed, Peckfield Colliery was located immediately to the south of the station platforms, complete with exchange sidings. A Class 37 resides in these whilst a 0-6-0 diesel shunts empty tippler wagons. (*24 July 1972*)

An NCB steam engine pushes loaded tipplers uphill to the spoil heap. The 'fireman' looks a bit young! (*24 July 1972*)

Glasshoughton's new station also required the construction of a new footbridge to connect its two platforms. (*4 August 2015*)

Much stonework, especially to separate itself from the large adjacent leisure complex, made this station relatively expensive to build, though the effect is attractive. (*4 August 2015*)

Knottingley's diesel depot (with Ferrybridge power station dominant on the horizon) used to have its own allocation of locos to work the numerous coal trains in the district. Nowadays its main task is wagon repairs. (*2 August 1974*)

Twenty-two years later, and post-privatisation, trainloads of coal were worked by National Power's Class 59s, though Ferrybridge remains the skyline's enduring feature. Taken on 3 April 1996, nearly a year after 59 203 had been named *Vale of Pickering*.

Weed-infested Pontefract Tanshelf has the favoured road overbridge means of getting between platforms, via sloping ramps. (*3 August 2015*)

A 2-car Pacer heads off to Monkhill. Trains are announced on the loudspeaker, rather than on an information screen. (*3 August 2015*)

Featherstone has staggered platforms separated by a level crossing, seen here half-raised, as the Pacer has already reached the platform. (*3 August 2015*)

Grand Central's trains from King's Cross pass through on their way to their Wakefield Kirkgate stop. (*3 August 2015*)

Streethouse's entrance is very much 'straight off the street', and the bus stop is right outside. (*3 August 2015*)

As at Featherstone, a level crossing provides access to either platform, though here these are not staggered. (*3 August 2015*)

Wakefield Line

Although the Wakefield Line is electrified through to Doncaster, the stopping trains to Sheffield divert via Moorthorpe and are therefore d.m.u.s. Hence, 142 066 has just called at Outwood on its way into Leeds from Sheffield. (*5 August 2015*)

Tracks at the north end of Outwood station turn sharply left; an overbridge closeby provides access to the platforms. (*5 August 2015*)

This is the 'Light Wave' at Wakefield Westgate, described in the text. A Class 141 Pacer waits its departure time further down the platform. (*23 March 1989*)

Westgate's station buildings, and those in the immediate vicinity, have undergone substantial alterations in recent years, some of which can be spotted in this view of a Sheffield-bound Pacer drawing into platform 1. (*5 August 2015*)

Virgin Trains East Coast run between Leeds and London every half-hour, so Westgate is a busy station. DVT 82 217 brings up the rear as yet another Leeds express departs. (*5 August 2015*)

South of Wakefield, the next new station is at Sandal & Agbrigg, where two Sheffield services have just crossed. (*5 August 2015*)

Here, to ring the changes, a pedestrian underpass allows access to the platforms. (*5 August 2015*)

Fitzwilliam is one of the earlier stations to be reopened on its old site. A Class 142 Pacer sets off for Leeds, with the footbridge connection in the background. (*5 August 2015*)

In summer both platforms are well hidden from view by mature trees. (And therefore plenty of leaves on the line in autumn!) (*5 August 2015*)

Off the electrified line, the first station is Moorthorpe, seen here on 23 March 1989, back when 'The Mallard' pub was still in business, and 150 262 was heading for Sheffield.

Hardly having left Leeds station, Holbeck engine shed appeared on the west side. A diesel depot at this time, 4 x 'Peaks' can be seen, and Classes 47 and 31 also attend. The 'viaduct line' crosses behind the 31. The site is still in railway use, but not as a depot. (*24 July 1975*)

Castleford has seen little in the way of improvements in recent years. Two tracks are visible, but the opposite platform is defunct, so that the repeated signage for platform 1 is superfluous as there isn't another! The proposed joint rail/bus interchange at this station hasn't happened either. (*23 October 2015*)

This is Normanton – an open station! The old has been demolished, but little of the rebuild has yet to materialise, though work is clearly in progress on 16 February 1988. Currently, Normanton enjoys an hourly service each way between Leeds and Sheffield via Barnsley.

The state of Wakefield Kirkgate has been transformed by the injection of large amounts of money (£5.6 million) in recent years. Predictably, it looks much better for it, even though it took about twice as long as originally planned. A southbound Class 158 Express unit gets under way from No.2. (*3 August 2015*)

Looking across from platform 1 to the island platform; a subway connects these. (*3 August 2015*)

The not-quite-finished exterior is not unattractive. 14 September 2015 saw the eventual completion of the work. (*3 August 2015*)

Berry Brow is the only single-track station to be opened under the West Yorkshire regime, so far. Lockwood station is only ¾ mile away, closer to Huddersfield, beyond the overbridge shown above. (*6 August 2015*)

This shot, looking south, was taken from the overbridge. (*6 August 2015*)

The branch to Clayton West hung on for years before final closure. The 12.10 from Huddersfield has just arrived at the rather run-down and very basic terminus. (*3 August 1974*)

The contrast with the station now named Clayton West could hardly be greater! The Kirklees Light Railway now operates from here, with splendid passenger facilities. (*25 March 2001*)

Looking in the other direction from the previous shot, a 3-road shed plus turntable confronts the eye, complete with two engines in steam! The green one is named *Badger*. (*25 March 2001*)

The blue 0-4-0 + 0-4-0 *Hawk* (a Kitson-Meyer articulated type built in 1998) was to power one of the trains; the red loco is *Fox*, a 2-6-2T built in 1987, and would work a second. (*25 March 2001*)

Coming out of Leeds, the first new station on this line is Cottingley where, relatively unusually, a new footbridge had also to be installed. Only local services stop here, and a busy evening service for Huddersfield departs formed of a Class 142 Pacer. (*4 August 2015*)

Dewsbury station is a Grade II listed building, and when seen here on 20 October 1974 still carried its 'Wellington Road' designation. (*20 October 1974*)

Mirfield once boasted a very substantial overall roof. (*20 October 1974*)

Another view of the extensive trainshed; long since demolished, but very distinctive. (*20 October 1974*)

Road tankers occupy the site of Mirfield's steam shed, as a 3-car Class 144 Pacer runs towards Huddersfield. (*6 May 1995*)

A little further west, one of the original Class 141 Pacers passes Heaton Lodge Junction. The viaduct in the background carried the Spen Valley line to Leeds via Gomersal. (*17 February 1992*)

Heaton Lodge Junction again, this time showing a Class 156 Super Sprinter in Regional Railways livery. The Calder & Hebble Navigation is in the background. (*17 February 1992*)

Two services do not normally stop at Deighton simultaneously, but here the Leeds train (platform 1) is late. A convenient road bridge provides passenger access to both platforms. (*6 August 2015*)

An overview from this bridge reveals two revenue protection staff awaiting the next train on platform 2. (*6 August 2015*)

The 10.17 Newcastle/Liverpool is about to depart (10 minutes late) from Huddersfield. The train description panel on the 'Peak' diesel matches exactly what was taking passenger traffic away from the railway to Manchester – the M62 motorway! (*26 April 1975*)

To change platforms at Slaithwaite the road underpass is used. Passengers are waiting for the Leeds train on No.1, viewed from the staggered platform 2. (*5 August 2015*)

Interesting artwork at the entrance to platform 1! (*5 August 2015*)

Bramley's staggered platforms are, like Slaithwaite's, accessed via a road underpass. Both platforms are (just) seen as a Bradford train exits platform 1. Next stop will be New Pudsey, where the original 1967 Park & Ride station building has been replaced (in 2013/14) with an up-to-date booking office and an even larger car park. (*5 August 2015*)

On 20 October 1974 Halifax looked like this. The usable platforms are on the right, with what remains of the Queensbury side of the station on the left.

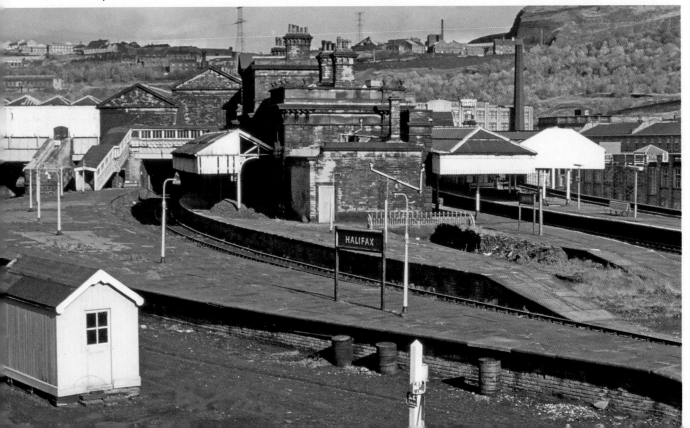

Thirteen years later, the station was already in an advanced state of decay, which wasn't rectified for twelve more years! This inviting scene shows a Class 150 ready to depart without further delay! Thankfully radical improvements have since been made. (*4 July 1987*)

Compared to the Huddersfield route, relatively little cross-Pennine freight used the Calder Valley line. However, here's a westbound coal train on Todmorden viaduct behind a Class 56; the panoramic view of the town is a bonus. (*25 July 1989*)

Walsden is the last outpost of the Metro system towards Lancashire, where the two platforms overlap and are connected by a footbridge of some vintage. (*7 August 2015*)

Low Moor, due to open during 2017, will become the first station out of Bradford Interchange in the Halifax direction. It is seen here taking shape on 6 July 2016; a footbridge (with lifts) will eventually join the near (westbound) platform to the one for Bradford. The station opened on 2 April 2017 to become the 26th new station on the Metro network.

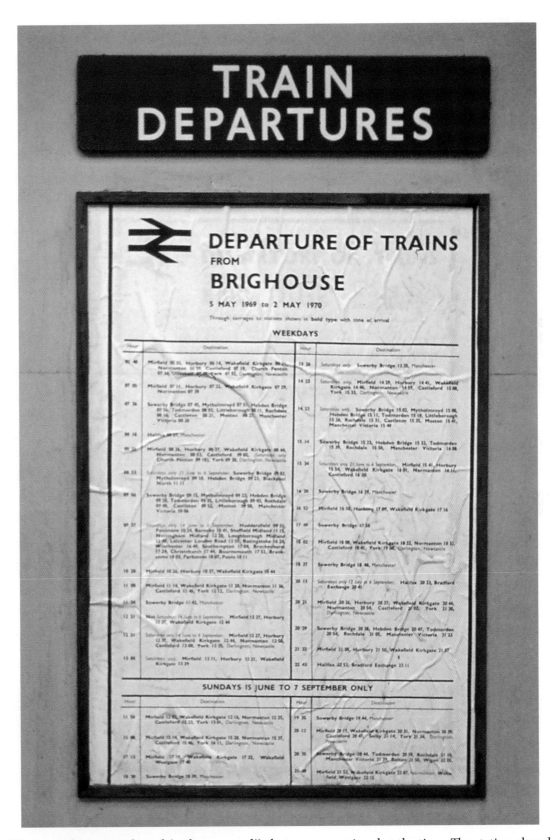

A view of the train departures board (rather creased!) that was operational at the time. The station closed during the currency of the timetable displayed! (*11 October 1969*)

Above: The new station is certainly more attractive than the old, with substantial floral displays on both platforms. Steps lead down from the road bridge, and the Halifax train awaits its departure time. (*4 August 2015*)

A long access ramp is required (or many steps!) to reach street level from platform 2. (*4 August 2015*)

A waste disposal train has Class 47 power on a misty day not far from Brighouse. (*15 February 1988*)

Considerable freight traffic moved in/out/through Healey Mills. A heavy load of coal travels near Healey Mills in private owner wagons behind a Class 56 diesel. (*19 February 1988*)

Healey Mills yard itself, with a large number of coal wagons in the sidings; the diesel depot is in the background and a Class 56 is also prominent. (*16 February 1988*)

A long train of Blue Circle Cement wagons leaves the yard with a 'Peak' in charge en route from Dewsbury to Hope (Derbyshire). (*16 February 1988*)

Chapter Six

What Next?

It is always difficult to draw definite conclusions from any set of data. However, the figures provided in the previous chapter certainly lend weight to the observations that, firstly, electrification does in itself promote increased patronage, and secondly that new stations (when suitably placed) also increase passenger numbers on almost any chosen line. Of the Metro network's twelve named lines, only the Hallam line and the Dearne Valley line (which has a limited service anyway) lack new stations, and notably, only four of the named lines are presently electrified.

So what further developments can reasonably be anticipated? The most obvious is the electrification of the cross-Pennine route from Manchester through Huddersfield to Leeds, York, Selby and Hull. York is already electrified throughout from London to Edinburgh, so that wiring the relatively short gap (20 miles or so) between Neville Hill and Colton Junction would not only create a direct electric connection from Leeds to the north-east and Scotland, but also an opportunity to run some King's Cross/Newcastle/Edinburgh services via Leeds. This scheme is of course already in the Government's thinking, and though a four-month 'pause' (June–October 2015) created some uncertainty, it does look as though this will happen, though the time-scale for completion may extend beyond the 'by 2019' deadline originally planned.

Five years later ('by 2024') it is also in the Government's thinking to electrify the Calder Valley cross-Pennine route to Leeds through Halifax and Bradford. These two routes are therefore the prime candidates for substantial expenditure in the next ten years, not only in infrastructure terms but also in new electric rolling stock. Once provided, this stock would, in theory, release diesel units to 'cascade' onto non-electrified Metro lines, allowing better quality stock to replace older vehicles.

In the same (electrification) vein, it is tempting to foresee Leeds/Harrogate/York being a candidate. Leeds to Harrogate is probably busy enough to warrant this, though the 20½ miles onward stretch to York is largely single track and this may count against such a decision.

Other than these just listed, it is difficult to envisage any further Metro lines justifying the expense of electrification. Outside these, and probably in the longer term, the route from Church Fenton to Sheffield may become a candidate, as and when the Midland main line is energised to reach Sheffield from the south. (The undecided routing of HS2 in the north of England may impinge on this thinking.)

At this juncture it is worthwhile listing the rolling stock currently available at Neville Hill with which to operate the twelve Metro lines. Of these, Classes 333 and 322 usually run the electrified lines north-west of Leeds; Class 321 units usually operate on the electrified Doncaster route. *Local* services on the non-energised lines are almost exclusively in the hands of Pacer Classes 142 and 144, whilst Classes 185 and 158 (plus some of the earlier 15x series units) predominantly run through and beyond the Metro boundaries on the two cross-Pennine lines.

Class	Power (hp)	Axle load (tons)	Max no. of seats	Year built	Max speed (mph)
2-car 142	460	12.3	122	1985/87	75
2-car 144	460	12.1	87	1985/86	75
3-car 144	460	12.0	145	1985/86	75
2-car 150	570	9.2	149	1986/87	75
3-car 150	570	8.9	240	1984	75
Single 153	285	10.3	72	1991/92	75
2-car 155	570	9.7	156	1988	75
2-car 156	570	9.9	152	1987/88	75
2-car 158	700	9.6	150	1989/92	90
3-car 158	1,050	9.6	202	1989/92	90
3-car 185	2,250	13.6	154*	2006	100
4-car 321	1,328	8.6	307	1991	100
4-car 322	1,328	8.6	291	1990	100
4-car 333	1,877	11.65	360	2000	100

* includes some 1st class accommodation standing room is of course available on all units!

So far as improving future carrying capacity is concerned, if rising demand is to be both generated and met adequately over the next 10–20 years, it is apparent that units of double the accommodation of the Pacer units (Classes 142 & 144) will be required. If/when the two cross-Pennine routes are electrified and their diesel units become available, 4-car trains (of two 2-car units) would be required from these to meet peak-hour demands, or possibly 3-car sets (Class 153 in combination with other units of Classes 15x). However, from the above table it is immediately obvious that, in comparison with electric units, the 15x series are underpowered, slow and in particular, already 25–30 years old! Additionally, the only other new(-ish) d.m.u.

listed above is unsuitable for local commuter work on the grounds of both seating capacity and axle load. Axle load matters; the Class 185 has an axle load 42 per cent greater than a 3-car 158 unit and this increases track maintenance charges. All the Metro lines are heavily subsidised by local and national governments, and *all* costs in the region must therefore be kept as low as possible. Unless newer commuter d.m.u.s can be cascaded (soon!) to West Yorkshire from other areas undergoing electrification (primarily the GW main line into South Wales), heavy refurbishment of selected existing Pacer and Sprinter units seems likely to be resorted to as yet another stop-gap measure. As West Yorkshire is all too familiar with these (as well as being 'guinea pig' for the original

141s), refurbishment of yet more old stock would not be a first choice. However, with additional electrification schemes being actively examined especially, it has to be said, in the north of England, the scope for new Classes of lightweight d.m.u.s with adequate life expectancy, speed, power and capacity to be of interest to the WYCA, would seem to be limited. It is therefore perhaps no surprise that Class 144e – the 'Evolution Pacer', a demonstrator unit put out on trials by Porterbrook – has been touring Metro lines from Neville Hill. It remains to be seen as to whether, ultimately, the economics of operation finally dictate this '2nd choice' option. Mobility legislation soon to be introduced will rule out continued use of Pacers in the near future; either these are replaced, or suitably modified to conform – which is what Porterbrook is trying to achieve with the 144e.

Both Northern and TransPennine Express franchises expired at the end of March 2016, the new franchisees Arriva Rail North and TransPennine Express (again) taking over as from 1 April. (See Appendix for details of their seven- and nine-year plans). The Government has recently introduced the idea of a 'Northern Power House' and hopes that these new franchises will play a significant role in boosting the economy of the entire region. There is also a consortium of twenty-nine local transport authorities known as 'Rail North' working on a twenty-year strategy to improve rail services provided by the two franchisees. Additionally there is a wider-ranging 'One North' scheme with a similar, but more detailed time scale, outlining specific targets to be met by 2019, then by 2024, then by 2026 and finally by 2030. These over-arching plans do of course include those of 'Rail North', but extend not only to new railway lines making connections with the proposed HS2, but also road/motorway improvements across the North of England. Just how all these fine schemes will play out around Leeds & Bradford only time will tell, but after the Eurostar, Heathrow Express, Docklands Light Railway, Thameslink, Crossrail and Bristol & South Wales electrification projects have finally run their course it's about time the North got a look in. Don't hold your breath however; future plans are always dependent on money (lots of it!) being available, and regional railways are, as mentioned above, heavily subsidised. The Department for Transport reported in 2011 for instance, that regional trains ran 19 per cent of the passenger miles nationally, but required 61 per cent of the Government railway funding to provide them!

Appendix

1.   **Bringing the development story up to date beyond November 2015**

2.   **Tickets from the Leeds & Bradford area**

3.   **Colour diagrams of Leeds station area before & after the 'Leeds 1st' rebuild**

1. BRINGING THE DEVELOPMENT STORY UP TO DATE BEYOND NOVEMBER 2015

2015

9 December	New franchisees announced.
	Arriva Rail North awarded the current Northern franchise for 9 years.
	First Group awarded the TransPennine Express franchise for 7 years, to be known by the same title.
	Both begin on 1 April 2016, and will be managed jointly from Leeds by Rail North and the Department for Transport. (See lower down for details).
13 December	Apperley Bridge opens (Airedale Line); first new Metro station for 10 years since Glasshoughton was added in 2005.

2016

4 January	Leeds station South Entrance opens.
31 March	Ferrybridge coal-fired power station closes after 50 years of operation.
April/July	New ticketing facility at Harrogate station; new concourse floor, better lighting and new waiting shelter complete £1 million refurbishment.
19 June	Kirkstall Forge station (Airedale Line) opens.

Detailed plans by the franchisees

Arriva Rail North has an ambitious programme of new trains within their franchise period, and will increase peak capacity by 37 per cent. Overall fleet size will increase from 771 carriages to 885, and all Class 142/144 Pacers withdrawn by the end of 2019. 281 new carriages (built in Spain by CAF) will be formed into 98 sets as follows:

> 43 emus (31 x 3-car + 12 x 4-car units) = 141 vehicles
> 55 dmus (25 x 2-car + 30 x 3-car units) = 140 vehicles.

All Class 153 railcars will be withdrawn, as will emus of Classes 321/322/323.
Additional dmus of Classes 150/156/158/170, and emus of Class 319, will be acquired to make up the new fleet by the end of the franchise.

TransPennine Express aim to introduce the following, thus taking on a notably InterCity approach to their franchise.

> 44 x 5-car sets with 125 mph capability delivered from spring 2018, of which 19 sets are to be Hitachi AT 300 bi-mode trains (electric/diesel), in traffic by the end of 2019. Other sets will be emus, and more orders have recently been placed to make up the 44 sets (i.e. 220 new carriages).

May 2016: further orders placed for the following new vehicles from CAF in Spain

> 12 x 5-car emu sets = 60 vehicles (the 12 'other' sets above) plus
> 13 x 5-car sets of loco hauled Mk5 carriages = 65 coaches.

The loco hauled sets will be headed by Class 68 diesels and will initially operate services between Liverpool & Newcastle (via Leeds) prior to electrification.

Additionally 29 x Class 185 dmus (out of 51 sets) are to be retained and extensively refurbished. The other 22 sets will be cascaded, as will their Class 350/4 emus and their Class 170 dmus. By 2020, 72 per cent of TPE's fleet will be new trains.

Both franchises intend to substantially increase Sunday services. Indeed TPE plan to match its Saturday and Sunday services with its off-peak weekday timetable from 2017! Rail North (a consortium of 29 Local Transport Authorities in the northern region) will monitor and deliver both of the above in conjunction with the DfT.

Other future plans already announced: dates still to be decided in most cases

- Feasibility work is in progress on the proposed new station at Elland.
- 11 Metro stations are to get extra free parking spaces, 800 in total to add to the 2500 already provided.
- VTEC also proposes extending some King's Cross–Leeds services to Harrogate from May 2019. (But not Ilkley!)
- Manchester/Huddersfield/Leeds/York electrified by 2024. TPE to run 6 fast trains per hour between Leeds & Manchester as soon as possible during its franchise.
- Improvements to Calder Valley Line to be made so as to be a diversionary route for TPE when Huddersfield Line closed for 6 tunnels to be electrified.
- Extra platform capacity will be made available at Leeds station.
- Huddersfield's £½ million refurbishment is now complete; three new waiting rooms plus a 1st class lounge (first for 60 years here, first on TPE's network), 54 bike spaces and improved car park lighting.
- From 11 July 2016 to December 2017 Arriva Rail North hires a Grand Central 5-car Class 180 to work an additional 07.43 Bradford Interchange/Leeds, a Northern service crewed by GC.
- Harrogate's £1 million upgrade is complete; two waiting rooms, new toilets, new seating and a new station entrance. Council also proposes through trains York/Bradford and Skipton/Knaresborough, via Harrogate.
- Smartphone ticketing to be trialled on Leeds/Huddersfield route. Both stations have ticket gates that accept the new technology.
- Leeds station's Wetherspoons pub could have a roof terrace added as part of a major refurbishment.
- Freight flows of scrap metal noted in Jan/Feb 2017, from European Metal Recycling's private siding at Laisterdyke to Liverpool Docks, and from Crossley-Evans' at Shipley to Cardiff Tidal.
- Halifax station and approach bridge to be demolished; replaced by two-storey building with access at ground level. £45 million proposal!

- Huddersfield receives highly unusual visit of Class 73s (73 962/73 963) top & tailing a Derby/Derby test train via Penistone.
- Upgrade of Manchester Victoria/Leeds via Calder Valley; next phase starts March 2017 between Todmorden and Bradford with track and signalling work.
- Leeds has £270 million plan for proposed new stations at (1) Bramhope (for Leeds/Bradford airport), (2) White Rose shopping centre, (3) Thorpe Park.
- Leeds aims for a redevelopment of its station as an integrated hub for HS2. South Bank regeneration initiative to provide 35,000 jobs and 4,000 new homes. Will report it's plans during 2017.
- Ravensthorpe station to receive refurbished shelters, and a new public information screen to be installed.
- WYCA expected to approve (in June 2017) a £15m plan to transform Forster Square station; main building rebuilt; new roof; new lifts; cycle storage; retail outlets. Public space created at entrance and scrubland landscaped.
- 7 June 2016 three trains pass over 3–4m of unsupported rail at Baildon due to washout. No derailment, but RAIB makes subsequent recommendations in 2017.
- Healey Mills yard made available by DB Cargo for train crash/derailment/fire training exercises, with all accident and emergency services present.

2. TICKETS FROM THE LEEDS & BRADFORD AREA

 1

 2

 3

 4

 5

6

7

8

9

10

11

1, 2   A couple of tickets from September 1969 with interesting consecutive serial numbers. (Is 00000 a number at all?)

3   A similar ticket from June 1972 had serial number 46248, which used to be the BR number for 'Coronation' pacific 'City of Leeds'! Note both the £ *s. d.* and decimal versions of the fare. (Britain decimalised on 15 February 1971)

4   By June 1976 when this was issued, Morley (Top) had closed (as from 2 January 1961) and Morley (Low) had been renamed plain Morley.

5   Platform ticket stamped 11 October 1969, three months prior to closure on January 1970. In May 2000 the station reopened as simply Brighouse.

6   A free ticket! The special occasion was the injection of 35 extra trains per day into the Leeds–Bradford (Exchange) timetable, making 52 in each direction, days a week, promoted by BR (Eastern Region) and WYPTE. All services called at New Pudsey where the car park had been doubled in capacity.

7   An Edmondson ticket issued in June 1972, but with decimal fare only.

8   On 23 September 1968 this single to Longwood cost 8*d*. The station closed as Longwood & Milnsbridge on 7 October 1968, only a fortnight later.

9   This fare-less ticket was issued in August 1968. Horbury closed on 5 January 1970 as Horbury & Ossett. 'Wakefield' refers to the Kirkgate station there.

10   Also purchased on 11 October 1969 (see 5 above) was this single to Halifax.

11   An interesting ticket; 3rd class was renamed 2nd class in 1956. Leeds (Central) closed in 1967, the Queensbury route in 1955, Low Moor in 1965 – but the ticket was issued on 23 February 1970 at double the printed fare!

Spot the difference

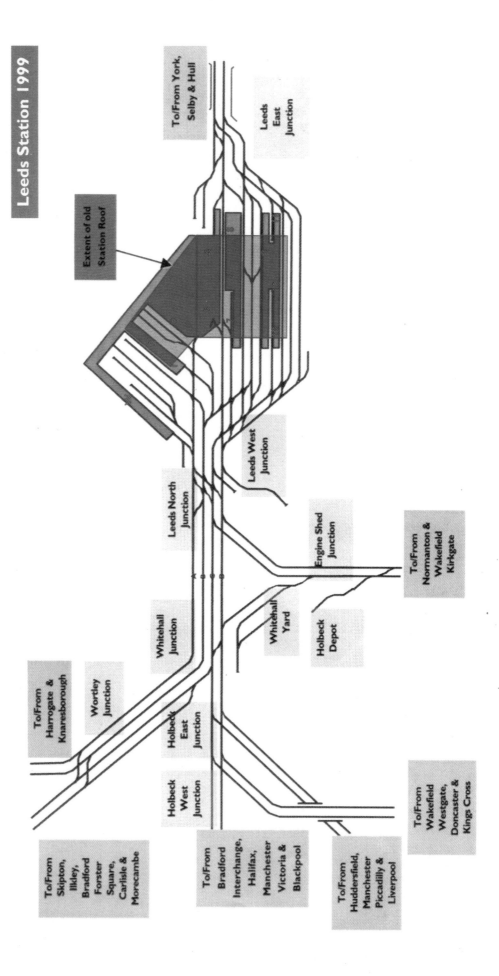

Leeds Station 1999

To/From York, Selby & Hull

Leeds East Junction

Extent of old Station Roof

Leeds North Junction

Leeds West Junction

Whitehall Junction

Whitehall Yard

Engine Shed Junction

Holbeck Depot

To/From Normanton & Wakefield Kirkgate

To/From Harrogate & Knaresborough

Wortley Junction

Holbeck East Junction

Holbeck West Junction

To/From Skipton, Ilkley, Bradford Forster Square, Carlisle & Morecambe

To/From Bradford Interchange, Halifax, Manchester Victoria & Blackpool

To/From Huddersfield, Manchester Piccadilly & Liverpool

To/From Wakefield Westgate, Doncaster & Kings Cross

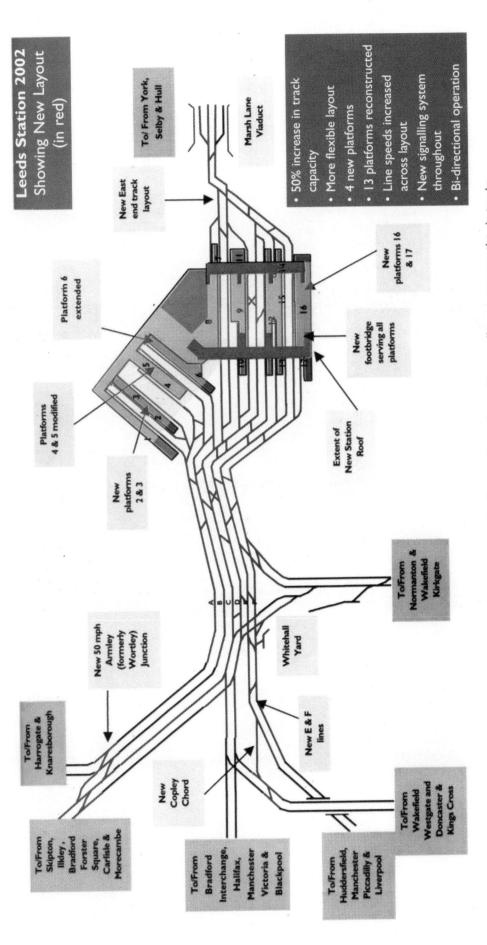

Leeds Station 2002
Showing New Layout
(in red)

To/From York, Selby & Hull

New East end track layout

Marsh Lane Viaduct

- 50% increase in track capacity
- More flexible layout
- 4 new platforms
- 13 platforms reconstructed
- Line speeds increased across layout
- New signalling system throughout
- Bi-directional operation

Platform 6 extended

New platforms 16 & 17

Platforms 4 & 5 modified

New footbridge serving all platforms

New platforms 2 & 3

Extent of New Station Roof

To/From Harrogate & Knaresborough

New 50 mph Armley (formerly Wordley) Junction

Whitehall Yard

To/From Normanton & Wakefield Kirkgate

New Copley Chord

New E & F lines

To/From Skipton, Ilkley, Bradford Forster Square, Carlisle & Morecambe

To/From Bradford Interchange, Halifax, Manchester Victoria & Blackpool

To/From Huddersfield, Manchester Piccadilly & Liverpool

To/From Wakefield Westgate and Doncaster & Kings Cross

With what is now effectively a 'grade separated' railway, train services will normally operate over the six tracks (shown A to F in the diagram) as follows:

A&B - Harrogate, Skipton, Ilkley, Bradford Forster Square, Carlisle and Morecambe

C&D - Bradford Interchange, Halifax, Manchester Victoria and Blackpool Wakefield Westgate and Doncaster to London King's Cross York, Selby and Hull

E&F - Huddersfield, Manchester Piccadilly and Liverpool to York/North East Castleford to Barnsley/Sheffield and Knottingley/Goole